THE SPRING OF SIGHT

THE SPRING OF SIGHT

An Inflection Point for Computer Vision and Society

Robert H. Boscacci

NEW DEGREE PRESS

COPYRIGHT © 2023 ROBERT H. BOSCACCI

THE SPRING OF SIGHT

An Inflection Point for Computer Vision and Society

ISBN

979-8-88926-953-3   *Paperback*
979-8-88926-994-6   *Ebook*

For Gianniboops, Panchi, Marko,
and Cece. This is all your fault.

CONTENTS

INTRODUCTION

Sure, you've used your laptop for video calls and taken heaps of photos with your phone. But what if our devices could truly *see*, like we do?

If you take nothing else away from this book, here is my general forecast: New tools and industries powered by computer vision (CV) will yield a net positive effect on humanity, but the key word is "net." There will be collateral damage, especially early on. As with any sufficiently powerful, general-purpose technology, there will always be ways to wield it carelessly or even with naked malicious intent—ranging from bullying to aiding in genocide. CV is no exception.

But what is computer vision, and how did we get here in the first place?

The universe still holds a great many mysteries, but few scientists disagree that human intelligence is a naturally occurring phenomenon. The process of evolution recurring over millennia prepared humans to wield tools. Our unique relationship with technology has, in turn, fed back into our evolution. If we had never harnessed fire, we wouldn't have consumed nearly as much protein, and our brains wouldn't have ballooned to their enormous size. Our capacity for reason owes a great deal to controlled fire, one of our earliest technologies.

As we fast forward through the last six thousand years or so, our species' most important tools have come to include such abstract concepts as money, written language, timekeeping, government, and most recently, software.

Within software lies the amorphous umbrella of "artificial intelligence" or AI. Apocalyptic headlines aside, AI is one of the fastest-growing fields of scientific and industrial research today. Global private investment in AI surpassed ninety billion dollars in 2021, more than doubling in a single year (Lynch 2022). Researchers have more than doubled their volume of academic publications in "pattern recognition" and "machine learning" since 2015, and "computer vision" has trailed closely behind those.

In this book, I'll use the terms "AI" and "machine learning" fairly loosely and interchangeably. Let's make the assumption, for the purpose of this short read, that AI is basically just a buzzword that entrepreneurs use to make their machine-learning-powered applications more marketable. This is not a book about the ongoing quest for "artificial general intelligence" (AGI) or "strong" AI. Those are theoretical systems with human-level capacity for learning and reason across many domains, or even full sentience. I use AI as a blanket term here, like you might in conversation at Thanksgiving.

Computer vision, one subset of AI, is quite like regular human vision but performed by computers. Before CV, you had to unlock your phone with a passcode; now you can just point its camera at your face to authenticate yourself. Before CV, the conversation around self-driving cars was purely hypothetical. The only way to diagnose and stage medical images was by showing them to an experienced radiologist or several. That has changed. Some forms of CV already live on your phone, and increasingly, it'll be built into our cities, automobiles, hospitals, and more.

Engineering computer vision systems has proven notoriously difficult because images can be so various and illusory. Our brains apply loads of post-processing to noisy visual stimuli after we've converted visible light into electrical impulses. Replicating that process isn't as simple as plugging cameras into computers. Putting boots on the moon was more straightforward.

Consider the act of catching a ball. It's natural to most able-bodied humans, but how would you train a cyborg arm and a couple of cameras to perform the same task?

First, the system would need a way to determine the velocity of the inbound ball. You may take your brain's inferential superpowers for granted, but by evaluating differences between the signals coming through your separate eyes over time and combining that with prior knowledge about the approximate sizes of known objects, you can estimate the trajectory of an approaching object in tiny fractions of a second. That's miraculous.

Next, your robot has to forecast an optimal time and place to meet the ball. The margin for error is relatively slim, even given a gentle toss, but the system can do some quick calculations given what it knows about the ball's velocity, the arm's possible range of motion, and its maximum mechanical reaction speed. Once the initial plan is set, the arm begins to move into place. This kickstarts a continuous autocorrecting loop. The ball gets closer, the visual signal improves, and the system fine-tunes its projected time and place of impact, finessing the arm's position.

Finally, the arm must shut its robotic fingers at the exact correct moment to trap the ball. The system needs to factor for the delay between the processing unit and the robotic hand's motors, so the "finger close" signal is fired a wee bit earlier than the ball is supposed to arrive at the planned point of impact. If all goes well, the fingers shut in the target position—just after the ball arrives, but before it bounces out again. Mission complete!

Beyond catching balls, can we train computerized systems to visually distinguish between baseballs and hand grenades? Between benign and malignant tumors? Between a mirage or an obstacle on the highway? What about between dangerous criminals and innocent bystanders? Between honest faces and lying ones? Between the faces of gay and straight people? Could computer vision systems help recruiters tell how suitable an employee you might be, compared to a hundred others, just by looking?

Critically: Even if they could, should they?

These sorts of questions inspired me to write this book. Together, we will explore this precocious branch of the AI tree, which is entering a new era of rapid growth. We'll discuss how computer vision will augment the fabric of our society, touching each of our lives, for better or for worse.

Computer vision exists squarely at the intersection between computer science and visual media. I spent more than a decade working in digital film production before making a career pivot into data science. I studied both computer engineering and film production at university, which is how I ended up working in a server room in the bowels of a New York City film post-production facility for several years and creating an automatic visual film slate (a.k.a. "clapper") detector with AI.

Technological progress follows certain patterns. As a species that evolves with our tools, we tend to:

1. Notice something natural

2. Attempt to bend it to our will, with some success

3. Experience painful second-order side effects

4. Smooth out the sharp edges

5. Start taking it for granted; rinse and repeat

Consider the discovery of fire. The standing hypothesis is that first, humans stumbled upon naturally occurring fires, foraging for conspicuously delicious, charred meat in the smoldering wake of infernos. Next, we graduated to purposely *spreading* fires, hoping the blazes would yield greater quantities of tasty snacks. We came up with reliable ways to start fires from scratch, using it for light and protection from predators. Humans experienced their fair share of burn wounds in the process of mastering fire, but once we figured it out, it became normal and ubiquitous. Today, we take fire for granted. Our stoves click on and off on a whim. Our combustion engines fire dutifully. However, we're already moving on: Electric motors and induction cooktops have started eating away at combustion's most direct applications in our daily lives.

Take nuclear fission for another example. This naturally occurring phenomenon took humans less than a decade to weaponize after its initial discovery. After Hiroshima and Nagasaki, a smattering of costly accidents further tainted the public's perception of nuclear technology as something inherently destructive, unpredictable, and corrosive. On the other hand, the energy density of nuclear fuel is "about one million times greater than that of other traditional energy sources" (US Department of Energy 2019). Nuclear energy is not without its risks, but if we're careful, it should make a handy stepping stone as we transition toward fully renewable energy sources.

I predict that computer vision will follow a similar story arc. In this case, *vision itself* is the natural phenomenon we're trying to bend to our will, and we're finally starting to experience a modicum of practical success. We're also starting to find ways to hurt ourselves with it, such as (further) enabling over-policing and discriminatory hiring. Now we have a choice to make. Our society can either keep experimenting until we stumble into every possible form of computer-vision-fueled self-harm, or we can use a little imagination, retrospection, and discourse to preempt some of that pain. Before long we'll be taking computer vision applications for granted, allowing them to serve as our chauffeurs and help make important health decisions because they'll be so much better than what came before.

Computer vision transcends the three-dimensional operations of robots in three-dimensional space. Nowadays, anybody can prompt a free online program for "a chair that looks like an avocado," and that program will cough up a few fairly convincing, arguably "original" images of chairs shaped like avocados. "Generative art" is taking on new meaning via computer vision. Its recent proliferation has reignited the debate around humanity's role in art in light of automation. Will visual artists' jobs get phased out? How will we compensate artists when their work is used to train generative art systems? Can humans use AI to win human art competitions?

A technological tool can be designed to look and feel more like a screwdriver or more like a gun. With a screwdriver in hand, everything looks like a screw; provided a gun, one seeks a target. The people and organizations developing computer vision technologies have a big influence on how the tools they build can be used—by way of the training data they assemble, the way they design the user interface, and the range of outputs they allow. We need to start holding organizations and individuals accountable for the potentially harmful computer vision tools they release into the wild, but that's impossible as long as computer vision stays on the outskirts of the public consciousness.

There's no reason for panic, but it's time to start educating and legislating. Folks in positions of power and from all walks of life should be tuned in to computer vision's potential so we can demand transparency and accountability from corporations, nations, and other centralized powers.

As computers get better and faster at processing and interacting with visual information, we must:

- Keep personal data private, especially people's faces

- Avoid creating "helpful" utilities that neglect underrepresented folks

- Stick to the scientific method, calling out snake oil where it appears

- Push for transparency at all levels, from underlying algorithms to the larger regulatory ecosystem

- Make computer-vision-powered tools more like screwdrivers than like guns

Once you know what it's capable of, you can help direct and focus computer vision's potential toward solving societal problems rather than further entrenching centralized powers. Let's provide people with the information they need to protect themselves in a world with ever more privacy pitfalls. Let's scrub away some of the mysticism built up around AI so we can be properly skeptical when it claims to be able to work miracles.

Think of this as a guided tour—from computer vision's origins in the sixties to today's state of the art and projections beyond it. In the chapters that follow, we explore the present and future of computer-vision-powered applications, like autonomous vehicles and medical diagnostic tools. We hear from the likes of MIT postdoctoral researchers and "solopreneurs" working from home, all at the cutting edge of their fields. Industry stalwarts weigh in on what keeps them up at night and what excites them. Policy experts weigh in on what advancements in computer vision will mean for the masses.

Welcome to *The Spring of Sight.* I hope you come away feeling emboldened to bring your lived experience and your voice to the chorus that will shape our collective future.

01

I SEE YOU

You've probably interacted with some form of computer vision in the last week.

It's easy to fixate on the dystopian elements of any new technology, but computer vision enables some helpful (and even, dare I say, delightful) applications. Let's have a look at how computer vision has already saved us from some tedious, hazardous, or otherwise impossible work.

Frequently, there's no better way to feed some real-world information to a computer than to simply let the computer see it. Analyzing image data is one of the most computationally difficult things that your smartphone can do today, but it *can* do it. Chipmakers' miniaturization of powerful computer processing components enables computer vision applications to seep into the very societal fabric around us day by day. The hardware required to extract rich meaning from images already fits in your palm.

Here in the early 2020s, what are the most commonplace incarnations of computer vision?

If you've ever used a selfie filter in a photo app like Snapchat or Facebook Messenger, for example, to transform yourself into a Pixar-esque cartoon character, you've seen computer vision at work. Locating facial landmarks, mapping the topography of your face, and applying amusing animations is a nontrivial image processing and augmentation task.

Speaking of your face's topography, if you unlock your phone with facial recognition, you're a frequent user of computer vision. Apple is reportedly testing a feature that will enable iPhone users to unlock their phones with Face ID even while wearing a surgical mask (Chadwick 2022). More than a billion iPhone users today stand to benefit from similar biometric-powered conveniences (Dean 2021). Your "faceprint" may become far more frequently used than your fingerprint as this capability matures.

A computer-vision-powered app called Pl@ntNet brings me closer to nature. Pl@ntNet gives me the ability to quickly identify and better understand any plant that I can photograph with my phone. Growing up in the suburbs, even as an avid weekend backpacker, I didn't spend much time familiarizing myself with the names and properties of the various trees, flowers, and shrubs in my surroundings. Now my phone works as my personal naturalist, and all it requires are images as input. The result is often a surprising and wonderful ecological learning experience.

On the Apple App Store, Pl@ntNet claims they make "it possible to recognize about 20,000 species. We are still a long way from the 360,000 species living on earth, but Pl@ntNet is getting richer every day thanks to the contributions of the most experienced users among you" (Cirad-France 2013). It's a pocket botanist and citizen science project, available for free to the roughly 85 percent of humanity that wields smartphones (Wise 2022).

In the same spirit, an app from Cornell's ornithology lab called Merlin Bird ID "learns to recognize bird species based on training sets of millions of photos" (Cornell Lab of Ornithology 2023). Granted, it's harder to photograph a tern than a fern with your phone, but this is still a boon for fledgling birders. Merlin has racked up over one million downloads on the Google Play Store; Pl@ntNet boasts over ten million, which is two million more downloads than there are people in New York City.

These two apps, Pl@ntNet and Merlin, are examples of image classification tools. You feed in an image, and the software does its best to classify the whole content of the image as this or that species of bird, tree, or whatever—usually within some limited scope. This classifying, bucketing, or discerning between different types of objects is one of the most foundational subtasks within the broader realm of computer vision.

Computer vision can do more than teaching us fun bird facts; it can make our societies safer. I'm grateful for the automated traffic enforcement cameras in my urban environment. As a bicyclist, I put my life in the hands of drivers every time I pedal to the library or farmers market. Biking on sidewalks is illegal in New York City for those over twelve, and bike lanes are often disjointed, so biking in the street with the freight and garbage trucks is standard practice. I'll take anything I can get in the way of additional safety measures, short of abandoning cycling.

In 2020 there were at least 6,343 crashes between bicycles and motor vehicles in New York City, resulting in 5,175 bicyclist injuries and twenty-four bicyclist deaths (NYC Department of Transportation 2021). Contrast that with only seventy motor vehicle occupant injuries and zero motor vehicle occupant deaths in those same crashes. Sheathed in literal tons of metal, cars have the obvious safety advantage on the road compared to cyclists. Computer vision, specifically OCR (optical character recognition), makes roads less hazardous for everyone by making people more conscious of their driving behavior.

OCR is the computer vision subtask of reading letters, numbers, and other symbols from images and transcribing them into neatly formatted digital characters. It's the automated equivalent of looking at symbols on a chalkboard (or a shipping container, or an old newspaper, or any analog medium) and typing them into a computer. I like to use the built-in OCR on my phone's photo app to extract tracking numbers from paper shipping receipts. OCR enables ATMs to validate the handwritten dollar amount on checks or archivists to digitize tens of millions of books, making them searchable. OCR has partly automated the issuance of automotive moving violations by enabling traffic cameras to read fast-moving license plates from a distance.

Automated license plate readers help locate stolen vehicles, monitor those with expired registrations, and generally pressure drivers to behave better. Speed cameras unequivocally reduce the average driving speed once they're installed (Wilson et al. 2010). These speed readings would be challenging to enforce if the cameras could not read license plates. The rub is in making sure systems like these aren't abused to impinge on our privacy; it's a delicate balance. Thankfully organizations like the ACLU exist to call "for the adoption of legislation and law enforcement agency policies adhering to strict privacy principles to prevent the government from tracking our movements on a massive scale" (American Civil Liberties Union 2022). They deserve more credit (and money) for that.

Speaking of road safety, computer vision systems in automobiles themselves have been saving lives—and tons of money for insurance companies.

If you've driven a car manufactured in the last five years, you've almost certainly used a form of CV. ADAS stands for advanced driver-assistance system. Between 2014 and 2020, equipping a vehicle with at least one essential ADAS feature like blind spot warnings, adaptive cruise control, or lane departure warnings resulted in 27 percent fewer bodily injury claims and 8 percent fewer collision claims on average (Kanet and Kohli 2021). Many of these features rely on CV. Some use radar, lidar, or ultrasound rather than typical visible light cameras. Tesla Inc. has stuck to a visible-light-focused approach, for better or for worse. In any case, as a bicyclist sharing the road with fast-moving multi-ton vehicles, I like to see CV-powered features making a quantifiable positive impact on safety.

How else do we use computer vision day to day, perhaps unknowingly?

Computer vision serves as an electronic Rosetta Stone. Google Translate was fantastically useful even before it boasted instant camera-based translation, but now it does that too. This feature "allows you to see the world in your language by just pointing your [smartphone] camera lens at the foreign text," which is "especially helpful when you're traveling abroad as it works even when you're not connected to Wi-Fi or using cellular data" (Gu 2019). This makes Google Translate one of the first and best examples of a truly useful augmented reality application.

It's magical to watch a block of text in an unfamiliar language instantly transform into something you can read and use. I wish I knew Japanese, Korean, and Arabic, but at least for now I have a way to decrypt the labels at my local Korean market in a pinch. Theoretically, in the not-so-distant future, your car's windshield could translate road signs from Icelandic into English or vice versa in real time, superimposing the translated text over the original. Computer vision makes the world smaller by giving us the confidence to travel and communicate where human translation might not be feasible.

Watching broadcast sports is becoming an increasingly computer-vision-intensive experience. Kinetic athletic data is useful to coaches, advertisers, networks, and fans. Given enough high-resolution game data, coaching staff can identify winning plays and patterns for specific scenarios. For example, as an NFL coach, I may value the ability to predict, based off the opponent's offensive formation, whether they're more likely to pass or run (Arastey 2020). Advertisers stand to gain metrics on which banner spaces appear more frequently on camera, and thus how they should be priced. Individual players and objects can be segmented in the image and automatically highlighted in replays, enhancing the viewing experience for spectators at home.

At the highest echelons of many sports, wearing sensors or tracking equipment inhibits movement, which is unacceptable to athletes. However, that doesn't curb the demand for more granular data. Metrics on player movement, ball/puck position, action recognition, and more are golden. Computer vision fills the gap that body-mounted sensors leave behind, estimating player positions, poses, and ball movement from the same broadcast footage that you and I watch on our screens at home.

When they're not watching football, Americans like to bolster their sense of home security. Faced with onerous fees for equipment, installation, and monthly service, many are turning to DIY home-monitoring and security systems. "At the end of 4Q 2018, 28 percent of US broadband households reported the presence of an active security system, up from 26 percent in 4Q 2017," according to a market research firm specializing in internet-of-things (IoT) industries (Parks Associates 2019). An increasing share of those households are protected by self-installed units touting "smart" features such as video doorbells, backup cellular internet and batteries, motion sensors, digital door locks, and more. These come with their own unique privacy risks, but properly managed, they give people a sense of security and self-sufficiency.

The IoT company Ring offers an innovative new feature for home monitoring: "Custom alerts work by having you train your camera on the two states you want it to recognize, such as when a garage door is left open or closed or when a car is in the driveway or not. The computer vision algorithm processes images of the scene...and sends an alert when it sees a change" (Tuohy 2021). Training computer vision-based classifiers is no longer just for programmers. It's baked into easy-to-use consumer electronics from mainstream manufacturers.

Computer vision liberates humans from tedious jobs in manufacturing, such as quality inspection, product assembly, and predictive maintenance. While human oversight will remain essential, humans get bored of rote work and burn out. I would rather burden software with the task of inspecting an endless deluge of glass vials streaming down a conveyor belt. It's nice to be able to take lunch while machines keep doing the boring stuff. Automation frees up time for people to learn new languages, make art, and track down more soul-crushing work to automate.

In health care, any minuscule improvement in efficiency can be a literal lifesaver. Computer vision shows promise in radiology, dermatology, cardiology, embryology, and other 'ologies. Medical image classifiers have been shown to call fewer false positives, detect tumors sooner, and make decisions faster than whole panels of radiologists with decades of experience. Clinicians stand to regain heaps of valuable face time with patients by working those systems into their practices—as long as patient safety and confidentiality are held paramount.

THE SPRING

Pl@ntNet and Merlin help me learn about my biome. Google Translate's camera functionalities bridge cultures. ADAS features and license plate readers make roads safer. Athlete and ball motion tracking supercharges the broadcast sports experience. AI-powered consumer electronics commoditize home security, and automated medical image analysis gives time back to overworked health care workers.

Computer vision has already made these constructive inroads toward the various corners of everyday life and many more. Increasingly performant automated visual processing systems will continue to augment swaths of industries, cities, and lived experiences. This continued proliferation marks a renaissance in the way we rely on image-oriented AI to work, learn, and create. We're bringing a sense of sight to systems that have historically been blind. Is it hubris to believe this development will do us more good than harm?

We've barely scratched the surface exploring computer vision's popular and potential use cases. Hopefully this small sample provides a baseline sense of the sorts of applications that fall under the CV umbrella. They typically exist at the intersection between cameras (or visual data) and software. They usually seek to replicate tasks normally performed by the human visual system. CV contains sub-disciplines like OCR, face recognition, ADAS and autonomous vehicles, image classification, and more.

Before we further examine computer vision's utopic and dystopic potential, let us glance back at the past. This is a fairly nascent field, but how far back does it go, exactly? Where did it all begin, and which characters gave life to this burgeoning discipline?

SUMMER VISION PROJECT

In a famous 1962 speech, President John F. Kennedy said, "We choose to go to the moon in this decade and do the other [difficult] things, not because they are easy, but because they are hard," crystallizing a sentiment of resilience and ambition, which resonated deeply with many Americans (JFK Library 2019). Less than a decade later, humanity stepped off the bottom rung of a ladder and onto the moon.

Fast forward to a data analytics firm in Times Square in 2019. A parody of that quote circulates between software engineers and eventually crosses my desk. This version more accurately reflects the eager naïveté with which the field of computer science has hurtled along since its conception: "We do these things not because they are easy, but because we thought they would be easy."

With that in mind, let's rewind again, this time to 1964. Seymour Papert, thirty-six, has been a research associate at MIT for about a year. It's possible that Kennedy's pioneering spirit has emboldened him and his colleagues at what will come to be known as one of the world's first and most prominent AI labs. He circulates a project proposal memo, something for the summer workers to wrap up before the fall semester begins: Teach a computer how to take some video input, and as output, describe what it's seeing.

What he's unknowingly asking his summer interns is, essentially, to please get started inventing the whole academic discipline of computer vision. The memo is titled "The Summer Vision Project."

With nearly six decades of hindsight, putting a man on the moon proved a more straightforward proposition. Bringing a full-fledged sense of sight to computers remains an unsolved problem in 2023, but Papert couldn't have known before he tried. Someone had to be the first to take a stab at this formidable host of engineering challenges.

Before his tenure at MIT, Papert is a young Jewish man living under South African apartheid. Raging against oppression, Papert earns a reputation as a radical leftist. He flees the country to avoid a fate in the same island jail in which Nelson Mandela spent the majority of his twenty-seven years of imprisonment. Papert's empathetic curiosity brings him to the field of educational theory and, in time, to become one of the founding figures in artificial intelligence.

It's natural to see someone like Papert, obsessed with human learning, pivoting into the nascent field of *machine* learning—even if the field isn't popularly called that for several more decades. Many great technologies imitate natural phenomena: Velcro is an imitation of the sticky burred seed pods that travel on the fur of animals (or your socks on hikes). High-speed Japanese trains draw aerodynamic inspiration from Kingfisher birds, whose streamlined beaks slide seamlessly into water (Green et al. 2019). Artificial intelligence and computer vision strive to mimic far more intricate natural phenomena.

Papert presciently approaches AI by first asking: What is intelligence, and how do children initially harness it? Infants begin life with only genetic instructions, receiving unfiltered, continuous stimulus from five senses. None of it makes any sense; there is no clear relationship between the lights, colors, sounds, smells, and comfort or pain. As babies, our brains are literally and figuratively squishy. Papert wonders: What exactly are the steps between this delicate, amorphous state and one where we can juggle bowling pins or execute an intricate figure skating routine?

Papert's vision memo circulates around the artificial intelligence group at MIT's MAC, the Project on Mathematics and Computation. This is a time of explosive energy at MIT. Some of the brightest minds in math and science amble the hallways, cross-pollinating ideas between psychology and theoretical physics. They vie for each other's research budgets and attention. J.C.R. Licklider, the "Johnny Appleseed of computing," moves on from his post at MIT's electronics research lab and embeds himself at DARPA in the Pentagon, where he successfully funnels two million dollars toward MAC's launch.

MAC starts out as a "project" instead of a "department" to skirt MIT red tape, making it easier to poach research staff from other departments. MAC earns the nickname "Switzerland" for its neutral position between departments. Papert's close colleagues there include John McCarthy, co-coiner of the term "artificial intelligence," and Marvin Minsky, whose work there establishes the foundation for artificial neural networks. Even the summer workers go on to become notable thought leaders and innovators in their own rights. On a quest to make machines more intelligent, MAC's AI group concerns itself with what it sees as the three key challenges on this new frontier: natural language, robotic motion, and vision.

Here are some excerpts from Papert's memo:

> The summer vision project is an attempt to use our summer workers effectively in the construction of a significant part of a visual system. The particular task was chosen partly because it can be segmented into sub-problems which allow individuals to work independently and yet participate in the construction of a system complex enough to be a real landmark in the development of "pattern recognition." The basic structure is fixed for the first phase of work extending to some point in July (Papert 1966).

As someone who still feels that computer vision is in its nascence in 2023, I cannot stress enough the magnitude of the hubris in this first passage. It is, however, simultaneously brilliant. Without much precedent, Papert and his group hammer out a roadmap, a gauntlet for the next generation of computer vision researchers to rail against for (at least) decades. They carry all the optimism of a generation that has just won a world war and will soon win the space race. Their blind optimism brings this effort to life, even if they're not bound to get it all done over just one summer.

> Sussman is coordinator of "Vision Project" meetings and should be consulted by anyone who wishes to

participate. The primary goal of the project is to construct a system of programs which will divide a vidisector picture into regions such as likely objects, likely background areas and chaos. We shall call this part of its operation FIGURE-GROUND analysis (Papert 1966).

Today Papert's "figure-ground analysis" goal goes by a new name—image segmentation.

Training a computer to take a whole image as input and return a label (such as "hot dog" or "not hot dog") is called image classification. In a 2013 online open-invitation competition, 213 participants from around the world trained their own image classifiers (using a set of 25,000 images for training) to distinguish between images of either dogs or cats. The winning model classified nearly 99 percent of the images correctly while sixty participants achieved a score of 95 percent or better (Cukierski 2013). That was nearly a decade ago. In 2023, image classifiers confidently bucket images into hundreds of categories, well beyond "cat" and "dog," and they do so much faster—or on cheaper, smaller hardware.

Segmentation, however, goes a step further. What is the exact shape of the object in the image? Which pixels belong to which object? To accomplish this, the machine has to classify every region within the image. Segmentation is one of the most active challenges in computer vision today. Papert gives a courteous nod to the complexity of vision, if not a complete one:

It will be impossible to do this without considerable analysis of shape and surface properties, so

FIGURE-GROUND analysis is really inseparable in practice from the second goal which is REGION DESCRIPTION (Papert 1966).

Papert correctly recognizes that light intensity, color, texture, and other hard-to-wrangle variables will have to be factored into any attempt to automatically distinguish objects within an image. He does not, however, appreciate quite how much variation there is, how much our brain filters and distills the firehose of visual information coming through the optic nerve.

The final goal is OBJECT IDENTIFICATION which will actually name objects by matching them with a vocabulary of known objects (Papert 1966).

Today this is called "object detection." Short of full image segmentation—with exact pixel boundaries—object detectors draw "bounding boxes" around likely "objects" and then classify and label each object. In one sector of the image, a fire hydrant; in another, a dog. You can imagine how this might be useful to an attack drone seeking tanks or a radiologist searching for tumors in medical scans. Papert continues:

Subgoal for July: Analysis of scenes consisting of non-overlapping objects from the following set: Balls, bricks with faces of the same or different colors or textures, cylinders. Each face will be of uniform and distinct color and/or texture. Background will be homogeneous. Extensions for August: The first priority will be to handle objects of the same sort but with complex surface and backgrounds, e.g. cigarette pack with writing and bands of different color, or a cylindrical battery. Then extend class of objects to objects like tools, cups, etc. (Papert 1966).

Today, nearly sixty years later, object detection is a largely solved problem. Even our phones have the capacity to isolate and identify specific elements within images. We can upload images to search for similar visual patterns on the web, extract and encode printed text, or automatically generate photo albums based on whose faces appear in pictures—all on the go. Free, general-purpose object detectors beckon to be fine-tuned for utterly specific purposes, like identifying subtle imperfections on medical vials.

Papert would be delighted with the progress we've made since his 1966 memo, even if he knew how long it would actually take, but would he be willing to hop into one of the robo-taxies ferrying passengers around San Francisco today?

03

MOTHERBOARDS AGAINST DRUNK DRIVING

When you drive a car, you rely heavily on your visual cortex—to avoid obstacles, read signs, and generally build a mental model of your surroundings. Likewise, no self-driving car would make it very far in the wild without some sense of sight.

Autonomous vehicles (AVs) are polarizing. Folks are typically either justifiably terrified at the thought of letting AI take the wheel, idealistic about self-driving's potential benefit to society, or some healthy mix of both. Regardless of where you sit on this spectrum, AVs and computer vision are tightly coupled. As computer vision advances, self-driving cars become safer and more feasible. In fact, computer-vision-powered features will be required in most new cars soon—whether or not people are still driving them.

It has been said that you don't have to outrun the bear; you just have to outrun your friends. Self-driving cars won't be absolutely flawless before they're deployed en-masse. They'll just be far safer than human drivers, and humans set a relatively low bar. However, this presents a chicken-and-egg situation.

How can we rigorously compare human drivers to AVs without first taking the risk of deploying them on the open road?

The most critical fronts in the war for self-driving market dominance include massive data collection and lobbying. On their quest to normalize and popularize AVs, auto-makers have to improve algorithmic computer vision frameworks, build colossal image-centric datasets, and fine-tune the logic around them, taking care to factor in nuanced, localized rules of the road. Self-driving has to *actually work*—demonstrably better than (at least teenage) human drivers—before the public is ready to let it roll.

While we take baby steps by implementing increasingly advanced driver-assistance features in most new vehicles, self-driving cars are already crisscrossing the United States, ferrying paying passengers around San Francisco, occasionally killing drivers and pedestrians, and generally promising (or threatening) to remove the need for human drivers.

THE PRONTO PRIUS

Some folks don't want to wait for the rest of us to be ready. Some demand the future now, at all costs.

In 2017, a headstrong former star Google engineer took a long drive. Starting at San Francisco's Golden Gate Bridge, he set out for a 3,100-mile, four-day voyage to New York City in a Toyota Prius, "in which he hoped not to touch the vehicle's controls except when he needed to gas up, pee or sleep" (Brekke 2019). This was supposed to be the first cross-country trip ever publicly conducted with driving automation technology.

The voyage succeeded. On October 30, the Prius sat in traffic on the George Washington Bridge between New Jersey and New York City, having transported its human supervisor to his destination without intervention or collision. The "vehicle was outfitted with advanced driver-assist technology developed by his latest startup, Pronto," which was "marketing a self-driving system for the trucking industry" (Brekke 2019). This feat makes the Pronto Prius sort of like the Apollo 11 of AVs—the very first of its kind. Mired in controversy, it was regardless a milestone that cannot be unachieved.

Why was it controversial? Perhaps because the Prius broke speed limits to keep with the flow of traffic. It made jarring maneuvers merging from on-ramps to highways. It stuck to the fast lane while cars passed in slower lanes to avoid complicated merge maneuvers. Nobody sought any special legal permission for this endeavor. The Pronto system was not nearly the safest, most courteous chauffeur to have ever traversed the country, but the time-lapse video of the complete voyage stands as evidence that it is nonetheless possible. The country has been irreversibly traversed by a self-driving car, with the caveat that it could not handle refueling itself.

In my lifetime, many more such autonomous journeys will follow. Not every such trip will be without incident, but ultimately, computer vision and its downstream applications will improve to the point where most rational travelers won't think twice about entrusting their lives to AVs. Robo-taxies will provide slower but more economical and comfortable long-distance transport than flying. A four-hour solo road trip could be spent working on a laptop, reading, or catching up on sleep, in a less fuel-efficient but more private experience than a self-driving bus.

You don't have to be a renegade software engineer to endow your personal vehicle with some self-driving capabilities. Ordinary consumers in regular cars can experiment with autonomous driving, at least in small doses, by purchasing and installing plug-in aftermarket gadgets like those offered by the startup "Comma.ai."

A twenty-something hacker named George Hotz started Comma. Their laconic mission statement is to "make driving chill" (comma.ai 2022). In a world where Tesla generates plenty of news and hype around their autopilot features, Comma quietly democratizes similar capabilities through open-source software and inexpensive hardware.

The most affordable Tesla sedan can be purchased new today in exchange for about half of the 2021 median annual American household income. It comes equipped with eight cameras for the car's spatial awareness. Per Tesla's website, their Autopilot feature "enables your Tesla to steer, accelerate and brake automatically within its lane" (Tesla, Inc. 2023). Drivers are supposed to stay alert and ready to take control of these critical functions at any time.

Comma's third-party equipment, which can be bought for less than two weeks of that same American household income, offers a handful of advanced driver assistance capabilities, but it works in any one of more than 150 supported cars.

Comma's system uses just two cameras. One faces forward, to see the road, and the other looks back at the driver, making sure they're alert. Per their public code repository, Comma offers such features as "Adaptive Cruise Control (ACC), Auto-mated Lane Centering (ALC), Forward Collision Warning (FCW) and Lane Departure Warning (LDW) for a growing variety of supported car makes, models and model years" (Hotz 2020). That's a significant enough subset of Tesla's Autopilot features to raise eyebrows and steal some potential customers.

How does Comma's gadget work in run-of-the-mill vehicles like the Prius?

> A model-specific wiring harness plugs into the vehi-cle's stock front camera behind the rearview mirror. That's where it taps into the car's communication network, which is used for everything from the power windows to the wheel-speed sensors. There it inserts new messages to actuate the steering, throttle, and brakes on its command (Vanderwerp 2020).

Did I mention that the codebase that powers these features, OpenPilot, is open source?

Open-source software is generally better for everyone than proprietary or closed-source code precisely because it's public. Anybody who cares to can access and inspect it, fix it, or even build and contribute their own new features. It's easier to trust something when you *can find out* exactly how it works, even if you don't actually take the time or don't have the special-ized technical knowledge to study what's under the hood. If a bit of open-source software is the least bit popular, people whose incentives align with yours (for example, those valuing passenger safety and data security) are likely to weigh in on it. This community effect is why Wikipedia works.

Comma.ai makes money not by keeping its algorithmic sauce a secret but rather by fostering this open-source codebase and selling the minimal computer hardware to run it in your car. That car could be a Honda, a Toyota, a VW, or any one of a number of other compatible models.

But how good is OpenPilot? *Car and Driver* wrote that they were "shocked at the sophisticated control of the system and its ability to center the car in its lane, both on and off the highway. Importantly, Comma.ai collects the data from the 2,500 units currently in use in order to learn from errors and make the system smarter" (Vanderwerp 2020). As with Tesla's Autopilot, we probably won't be able to trust Comma's Openpilot to manage the relative chaos of city driving for at least another five to ten years, but it's nice to know that the self-driving market isn't headed toward a total monopoly. Low-cost systems that do an impressive job gassing and braking through stop-and-go rush-hour freeway traffic are available now.

This type of grassroots, partly crowdsourced disruption is important for a healthy marketplace. Every technology has a "Promethean" moment, where some knowledge is stolen from the proverbial Mount Olympus and brought down to the masses. Venkatesh Rao writes about how "software as a Promethean technology emerged in the heart of the industrial social order, at companies such as AT&T, IBM and Xerox...but its Promethean character was unleashed, starting with the early hacker movement, on the open internet and through Silicon-Valley style startups" (Rao 2015).

Technologies born in ivory towers become truly important when the masses are allowed behind the curtain to bend it to their will. That's what Comma is doing for AVs. Just as the iPhone and iOS met their Promethean foil with the advent of the open-source Android mobile operating system, so will self-driving systems, powered by computer vision, continually trickle down from centralized powers like Tesla and GM into the hands of the many.

LEVELS

Society won't leapfrog from fully human-operated cars to fully self-driving cars overnight. A number of intermediary technologies are bridging the gap to an increasingly autonomous automotive future, some of which drivers around the globe already take for granted.

The Society of Automotive Engineers (technically "SAE International" now) develops international standards for the engineering professionals working on bridging that gap. This is the same society that invented the automotive "horsepower" metric. In 2021, aiming to unify the language around AV development, they published a "Taxonomy and Definitions for Terms Related to Driving Automation Systems for On-Road Motor Vehicles" (SAE International 2021). The specification details six levels or tiers of driving automation. On the bottom end of the ladder, "level zero" systems provide, for the most part, momentary warnings and assistance, whereas the top "level five" systems theoretically completely remove the human from the driving feedback loop.

I learned to drive in a car with two brake pedals. One was for me, the student, and the other was for my high school's driving instructor in the passenger seat. With a rotating cast of sweaty, pimple-faced fifteen-year-olds behind the wheel, that instructor needed some small shred of disaster mitigation capability for basic survival. Computer vision promises to serve as that second guardian brake pedal for the rest of us, for the rest of our driving years.

Automatic emergency braking (AEB) falls under SAE level zero. Once it's perfected, it will bring us one giant leap closer to realizing full self-driving. At the very least, an AV should be able to stop when an obstacle appears in its path. AEB is still relatively young, but "more than twelve major automakers equipped nearly all their 2021 vehicles with automatic emergency braking...a technology that has been proven to reduce crashes and injuries by stopping or slowing a vehicle if a collision is imminent" (Barry 2021). Cars equipped with AEB today still experience some false positives and false negatives—emergency-braking when they're not supposed to or vice versa—but it will only improve and become more ubiquitous over time.

While engineers hammer away at increasing AEB's reliability, risk-prone ex-Googlers cross the country in Toyotas equipped with level two or three systems. In San Francisco, traffic cops have pulled over compact SUVs only to find no humans inside. Those are today's level four systems.

Here are the various SAE levels delineated in slightly more detail:

Levels zero through two require you, the human driver, to *drive*, to be the one primarily responsible for the driving. You "must steer, brake, or accelerate as needed to maintain safety" (SAE International 2021). Levels three through five do not.

In level zero systems, lidar or other sensors may detect that a vehicle is in your blind spot and alert you with beeping sounds if you signal to change lanes in that direction. The car's built-in rear-view parking camera may keep track of your position between lane lines and warn you (again with beeps, and perhaps some flashing lights) when you stray too far from the center of your lane. A forward-facing radar may detect when a frontal obstacle is approaching too rapidly and engage the brakes without the driver engaging the brake pedal. Traditional cruise control is not sophisticated enough to make the list of driver support features that might constitute level zero driving automation.

In level one, the lane departure warnings from level zero may mature into automated lane centering—in other words, steering support. The driver need not make fine adjustments on the steering wheel to keep the car centered in its lane on the freeway. Alternatively, or additionally, the vehicle may feature adaptive cruise control, which, unlike regular cruise control, engages the brakes and attenuates acceleration to accommodate forward traffic. It does so by using radar, lasers, cameras, or some combination of several such vision-based sensors. If a vehicle is equipped with both smart steering *and* brake/acceleration support, it is considered a level two system.

At level three, we cross a threshold where the human behind the wheel is no longer the primary driver—at least not when the automated driving features are engaged. A level three system may request human intervention more or less frequently, such as when the car is in a chaotic or totally off-the-grid situation. In straightforward scenarios such as freeway traffic, the car may be able to pilot itself without intervention for longer stretches.

Level four systems require no human intervention. A perfect level four system could be set loose in some confined (and probably thoroughly mapped) geographic boundary, such as the city of San Francisco, and trusted to safely ferry passengers around town. There's not much reason for a truly level four system to feature a steering wheel.

Level five features take level four's functionalities beyond constrained geographic boundaries. A level five system could pick up a skier in Manhattan before dawn and deliver them to a mountain in Vermont in time to catch the first chairlift—or perhaps further north, to visit with family in Montreal by the evening.

Now that we have a taxonomy of the capabilities and accompanying engineering challenges ahead of us, we can forge on implementing them and carving out the requisite regulatory guardrails to do so in a safe way. Proactive regulation is entirely necessary in this budding arena because not every company will put consumer safety before shareholder value.

COSTS

No technology is perfect, but the consequences of flawed computer systems are magnified when they're encapsulated in literal tons of metal and loosed on public roads. What kind of damage have self-driving cars done so far?

As of this writing, nobody has died yet inside a "real" (SAE level four or five) self-driving car; not many are on the road yet in which to die. However, a growing number of people have perished (perhaps, at times, by placing too much faith) in level three systems. In at least one instance, an experimental level four self-driving car struck and killed a pedestrian.

Early in 2018, a self-driving Volvo, a prototype operated by the ride-sharing company Uber, ran over and killed a pedestrian in Tempe, Arizona. This "was believed to be the first pedestrian death associated with self-driving technology," and thus a sobering moment for technological optimists (Wakabayashi 2018). The backup driver at the wheel failed to take action to prevent the car from striking the pedestrian. Uber "quickly suspended testing in Tempe as well as in Pittsburgh, San Francisco and Toronto" (Wakabayashi 2018).

Self-driving systems hold the promise to make roads safer for everyone eventually, but they will inevitably incur casualties along the way. What price, in human lives, are we as a society willing to pay in order to bring AVs onto the open road? Where else can these vehicles practice collecting feedback and becoming more perfect driving systems?

Each individual human life is invaluable, but what if mature AVs carry the promise to save countless lives (from, say, drunk drivers) down the road? The moral and legal battles around this issue will intensify as AVs proliferate and do more harm to property and human bodies.

Tesla is infamous for bringing level three features to a broad consumer base, perhaps too early for their own good. Their Autopilot feature has come under heavy scrutiny in recent months as more Tesla drivers and their passengers have met untimely deaths. Tesladeaths.com presents visitors with a detailed spreadsheet. Columns include date, country, state, number of deaths, Tesla model, autopilot claimed, and more. A source column has links to news pieces detailing each tragedy.

During this book's editing process alone, the number of "autopilot claimed" deaths on that sheet climbed from twenty-five to thirty-eight. Those are fatalities in which someone claimed that Tesla Autopilot was at least partly to blame for the incident. The number of "confirmed Tesla autopilot crashes" climbed from twelve to nineteen; those are instances in which Autopilot was active during a Tesla crash involving at least one death (Bachman and Capulet 2022).

Headlines on this sheet include "Two People Killed in I-75 accident after a Tesla crashed into a parked tractor-trailer"; "Motorcyclist dies in I-15 collision with Tesla on autopilot"; and "Feds probe New York Tesla crash that killed man changing flat tire." That last article mentions that "Tesla has been criticized by the National Transportation Safety Board and others who say it needs a stronger system to watch drivers to make sure they are paying attention" (Krisher 2021). This is where regulators shine—when a technology gets ahead of itself to the point where it hurts people. Tesla may be doing more harm than good by deploying impressive but half-baked autonomous driving features in a reckless push to cement themselves as the frontrunners in this nascent domain.

BENEFITS

The potential savings in human lives (and dollars) that AVs could bring are considerable. Analysts at consulting firm McKinsey & Company made some back-of-the-napkin projections a few years ago:

By midcentury, the penetration of autonomous vehicles and other ADAS could ultimately cause vehicle crashes in the United States to fall from second to ninth place in terms of their lethality ranking among accident types. Today, car crashes have an enormous impact on the US economy. For every person killed in a motor-vehicle accident, eight are hospitalized, and one hundred are treated and released from emergency rooms. The overall annual cost of roadway crashes to the US economy was $212 billion in 2012 (Bertoncello and Wee 2015).

Automotive safety is steadily improving on aggregate, but collisions are still a massive plague. In 1970, roughly sixty thousand souls perished in automotive collisions in the US. That number fell to just above thirty thousand by 2013. While that's an improvement, it's still nowhere near zero, which is the hypothetical ultimate goal. Globally, as of 2018, "the number of annual road traffic deaths has reached 1.35 million...road traffic injury is now the leading cause of death for children and young adults aged five to twenty-nine years...it is the eighth leading cause of death for all age groups surpassing HIV/AIDS, tuberculosis and diarrheal diseases" (World Health Organization 2018). People's eyes tend to glaze over at metrics like these, but they're worth internalizing. Safer vehicles with more robust ADAS features will play a key part in improving abysmal statistics like these.

A report prepared for the US Congress breaks down critical reasons for car crashes attributed to drivers (National Highway Traffic Safety Administration 2008). Of these crashes, more than 40 percent occur due to recognition errors like inadequate surveillance, internal distraction, and daydreaming. Many more (more than 24 percent) are decision errors, such as driving too fast for the conditions, too fast for a curve, making flawed assumptions about another's actions, making illegal maneuvers, and so forth. Self-driving cars equipped with computer vision will make far fewer of these sorts of mistakes once we get them dialed in. Computer systems are either on or off, consistently either performant-enough or not yet passable. They do not daydream.

Humans are irrational and unpredictable. That is as true on highways as it is at a poker table. Motherboards don't drive drunk. Silicone transistors don't underperform after a thorny romantic breakup. Computer vision systems aren't affected by poor sleep. Hence, I propose the genesis of a new organization dedicated to promoting the widespread adoption of AVs for the safety of future generations. It could be called Motherboards against Drunk Driving.

PROGRESS

As a new father, Paul Filitchkin takes a personal interest in making American roads safer. His job as a data scientist involves fusing thermal vision cameras with regular visible light to improve automatic emergency braking. He told me, "The state of the industry right now is these [AEB] systems on consumer cars...just don't work very well. Maybe they work okay during the day, but they fail completely at night or in various bad weather conditions. And so for me, the immediate goal is just making sure to release a system that has relatively high precision." Adding heat-vision to the sensory stew can drastically improve performance in such adverse conditions as fog, snow, and direct sun. This hybrid approach is rare today in consumer cars, but I'd wager that such hybrid systems will be commonplace well before 2030.

The political winds appear to blow in Paul's favor. In 2021 the $1.2 trillion Infrastructure Investment and Jobs Act included provisions for "supporting the safe testing of automated vehicle technology and any preparation necessary for the safe integration of automated vehicles onto public streets" and also to "improve transportation infrastructure design in anticipation of increased usage of automated driving systems and advanced driver-assistance systems" (US Congress 2021). Big money is earmarked for projects demonstrating the use of automated transportation, sensor-based infrastructure, and commerce logistics supporting efficient goods movement. It even has language in favor of exploring connected vehicles, which would send and receive information about vehicle movements between neighboring cars on the road.

Title IV directs the "DOT to implement rules to establish minimum performance standards with respect to crash avoidance technology and to *require on all new motor vehicles* forward collision warning and automatic emergency braking systems, and lane departure and lane keeping assist systems" (US Congress 2021). That's not a suggestion. It's an order! Our political system is well on its way toward making sensor-assisted technology required in consumer cars, and full self-driving is not much further over the horizon.

DATA DRAG RACE

Today's frontrunners in the AV business include Waymo (which started as Google's self-driving car project), Tesla (much maligned in the news), and Cruise Automation (now a part of General Motors). Amazon has entered the fray with the acquisition of Zoox, and Apple reportedly has their own self-driving car in the works (O'Kane 2021). How do we know which competitor is truly in the lead?

One metric to watch is the number of real-world miles collectively driven by each organization's fleet. All of these market players are fervently amassing behemoth troves of real-world driving data with fleets of varying size experimenting in the wild. The idea is to expose the vehicles to as many unique and nuanced driving scenarios as possible so eventually no situation will seem completely novel. With enough shared experience under their belts, AVs should be able to basically mix and match situations they've seen in the past to handle unseen experiences in the future.

If GM's fleet has only amassed five hundred billion cumulative miles of practice, and Waymo has amassed more than a trillion (hypothetically speaking; these are imaginary figures), then hypothetically you should feel safer in one of Waymo's driverless robo-taxies. But what about the qualitative nature of those miles? How many were densely populated city miles versus interstate highway miles? How many were driven through adverse (wet, dark, foggy) driving conditions? Did the vehicles encounter enough bizarre situations, such as stop signs with exceptions (e.g., STOP—EXCEPT RIGHT TURN)?

In 1975, British economist Charles Goodhart famously postulated that when a measure becomes a target, it ceases to be a good measure—and "Goodhart's law" has proven itself many times over since. If the raw number of miles driven becomes our de facto measure of a self-driving system's confidence and safety, the central players will find ways to game that metric. We must look further to properly evaluate and regulate AVs.

Tesla hopes to solve self-driving by relying solely upon the visible light (regular) cameras built into their cars. Most other companies depend upon much more expensive lidar sensors to make high-precision three-dimensional point-maps of their environment. If Tesla succeeds, they will have a much lower-cost solution to the problem. If they do not, the price of lidar sensors should eventually decrease as manufacturers ramp up production to address the resulting increase in demand.

TROLLEY PROBLEMS

The trolley problem has many variations but is approximately the following thought experiment.

A train hurtles down the tracks. In its path are three people, stuck to the railroad ties. You have the option to pull a lever to redirect the fast-approaching train to an alternate track, where it will instead strike only one person (also stuck). Do you pull the lever, saving three people and killing only one instead? Or do you remain inactive, leaving three to die without inserting yourself into this tragic scenario? This has been the subject of much moral debate since the mid-twentieth century.

Similar situations could theoretically happen in cars on the road. In a fast-moving car, should you, the driver, (A) continue straight and plow into the previously obscured bicyclists, or (B) save them by veering off of a steep cliff, to your own demise? In a human-operated car, this would be a split-second decision, limited by the relatively slow speed of the human nervous system. But what about in an AV, where reactions to situations are sort of pre-programmed and nearly instantaneous?

Software engineers working on AVs are not writing explicit rules for every hypothetical scenario that could ever occur in the wild. While explicit rules with regard to traffic laws certainly exist (for example, "stop at stop signs"), autonomous driving systems operate on largely probabilistic terms. Like humans, AVs make observations about the world around them, make their best guess about where nearby objects will be in the near future, and attempt to minimize risk while progressing toward their destination. No block of code details which is the lesser of two evils. Faced with the wildly improbable hypothetical scenario outlined above, an AV would probably just recognize a forward collision avoidance scenario and slam the brakes.

I asked Dr. Ramin Hasani, a postdoctoral AI researcher at MIT, about the trolley problem in the context of self-driving cars. He told me, essentially, that there are more pressing things to worry about:

> The way we're designing autonomous vehicles, auton-
> omous systems, and intelligent agents, they would be
> less probable, by far, to end up in a trolley problem kind
> of situation. Usually, you end up being in those kinds of
> morally challenging situations when you have a human
> driver, when you have a lot of arbitrary behavior. Ulti-
> mately, fifty years from now hopefully, we won't have
> any human drivers. Fifty to one hundred years, let's say.
> If you don't have any human-driven cars, I think that

would be much better because the uncertainty of the whole world is going to decrease significantly. Then we wouldn't end up having those kinds of dilemmas.

American roads will be safer when the entities piloting the vehicles can't be distracted by text messages, dogs, nor fussy children. If removing human drivers from the equation entirely will make our roads safer, how do we get there faster? Which speed bumps will we hit along the way, besides the obvious technical challenge of making AVs reliably performant and safe? Dr. Hasani believes that public relations, in the most genuine sense, will be key.

What matters most is to prepare the public in general, or people who are machine learning outsiders, to much better understand the process that we are going through designing these algorithms. For that, we need interpretability, we need fairness analysis, we need ethical analysis of systems, and we need accountability analysis. This has to be open source and at the level of understanding that people from the science community, from other communities, can understand—the general public. They should understand how we are designing a system, and that this is not just a plug-and-play black box that we just let run in the streets because it is actually not like that.

Hasani's ideas underscore the importance of initiatives like Comma's open-source autopilot. Autonomous driving can't remain shrouded in mystery, as an industry secret or marketing gimmick, if we plan to deploy it at scale. It needs to be open and available for the public to dissect and improve, or at the very least for regulators to evaluate in detail.

IN MY LIFE

Here in 2023, I am thirty-one years old. Wilderness backpacking is one of my favorite ways to spend a long weekend. It feels safe to project that during my lifetime, I will get the chance to commission a robo-taxi to ferry me and my companions from the city to a remote forest trailhead or at least most of the way there.

Robo-taxies will have little trouble navigating well-mapped urban areas and most common paved highways. I may still have to take the helm once we're way out in the boonies, where asphalt gives way to dirt paths and obscure backroads. Computer vision is a data-hungry flavor of AI; I would not expect this automated system to have enough off-grid experience to properly navigate the last bumpy mile or two before the trailhead. Perhaps my forecast is too conservative. Perhaps once we've been dropped off at the trailhead, our ride will reverse itself back out through that same dirt path to go ferry around other passengers. I'd love for it to circle around and pick us up in a couple days, on the opposite end of our one-way through-hike.

04

IN SILICO

As pleasant as it may sound to live in a world where anybody can afford a safe and efficient algorithmic chauffeur, it will be even nicer to live in a society with an (even marginally) un-fucked medical infrastructure. Despite the heights we've reached in modern medical technology, not to mention the many capable and well-intentioned folks working in the field, today's American health care system is a shameful, labyrinthine minefield of predatory insurance policies and accessibility shortcomings, further ravaged by the recent pandemic. AI isn't going to fix all that, but the system needs help from wherever help can come.

Eric Topol's *Deep Medicine* gives a panoramic view of the myriad ways in which AI will give precious time back to clinicians. He posits that AI will liberate doctors, nurses, radiologists, and others to be more present with patients and thus deliver better health outcomes. I highly recommend Topol's text for an expert and holistic look at the broader AI landscape in medicine, but here I'll provide a distillation of just the most salient bits touching on computer vision—excluding other AI subtopics like natural language processing, speech recognition, and handling tabular (spreadsheet-like) data.

The clinical world is fighting a war on many fronts. Those fronts include:

- Clinician burnout
- Rampant misdiagnoses
- Inefficiency, such as superfluous testing
- Corporate greed
- Outdated record-keeping systems

These sorts of problems are not mutually exclusive. They feed into one another in malicious loops.

My partner is a board-certified genetic counselor. Every morning for several pandemic-riddled years, Catherine walked through slushy winters and muggy summers to her post at a nearby hospital. She loved helping Brooklyn's patients order and interpret the genetic testing they needed to make informed decisions on topics from maternal health to oncology. Her best days at work always involved interfacing directly with patients, making sure they were informed and empowered. Disappointingly, however, the hospital ultimately failed to support her mission to provide adequate genetic testing to the local patient population.

Through Catherine, I observed second-hand how logistical shortcomings can get in the way of quality health care. Clinicians around her struggled with continuously ballooning responsibilities. The best employees churned out under pressure at an astounding rate. Nepotism in the administrative hierarchy ran unchecked. One particularly old-school, heavy-handed breast surgeon earned an unsavory moniker: "the butcher." Frustrated and unable to provision the administrative resources required to provide adequate care for her patients, Catherine jumped ship. She works at a private genetic testing lab company now, where she can do meaningful work and remain shielded from the hunger games of the purely clinical world.

A big part of what drove Catherine out of the clinic was systemic inefficiency. Various practical plagues robbed her of time and mental energy that could have been better spent directly with patients. Picture rickety filing cabinets jammed full of disorganized (but probably critical) historical patient records. The hospital mailroom consistently misplaced outgoing test kits, forcing patients to return for replacement blood draws. Catherine frequently had to jockey for private space in which to conduct sensitive counseling sessions regarding patients' cancer and reproductive histories. The list goes on.

Pragmatic headaches like these should sound relatable to anybody with a personal connection to a clinical worker, especially after the COVID-19 crisis of 2020. Not all such problems can be magically remedied with AI and computer vision, but it's time to explore some new ideas for the clinic.

As computer vision evolves from academic curiosities into real clinical tools, it offers some lofty promises, but these boons are not without their countervailing pitfalls.

Provided that scientists and regulatory bodies collaborate effectively to minimize the pitfalls in the short term, computer vision automation tools have the potential to improve health outcomes for untold swaths of humanity in the long run.

Topol believes new tools like computer vision-powered radiology will become more commonplace. He writes that the "workflow will improve for most clinicians...by faster and more accurate reading of scans and slides, seeing things humans would miss" (2019). But what will become of specialized workers like radiology technicians, whose careers are partially built on the unique ability to interpret medical scans?

One of the central takeaways from *Deep Medicine* is that "to take humans to the next level, we need to up our humanist qualities, that which will always differentiate us from machines. Notably, human empathy is not something machines can truly simulate." If a machine steals your job classifying blobs in CT scans, your new job will be to run that machine skillfully and to deliver the results to patients with as much clarity, empathy, and humanity as possible.

CLINICAL PAIN POINTS

Where are our medical institutions hurting most?

Misdiagnoses are alarmingly common in our health care landscape. Topol points to studies that found "more than twelve million serious diagnostic errors each year in the United States alone" and the striking statistic that "most people will experience at least one diagnostic error in their lifetime" (2019).

My grandfather could have lived another decade or more, except his cancer went undetected for months as it metastasized. You and your family shouldn't have to go to the nation's most prestigious cancer institutions just for accurate diagnoses. We have the technology to treat increasingly malicious conditions, but only if they're correctly identified in a timely manner. Access to early detection is critical for everyone.

Radiology is one area where diagnostic tools need particular attention. Doctors and technicians spend loads of time staring at slides, debating whether or not a certain region may or may not warrant further investigation. Often, they come to the wrong conclusions. As far as Topol knows, "there is no system in place for doctors to get feedback on their diagnostic skills during their careers," and "31 percent of American radiologists have experienced a malpractice claim, most of which were related to missed diagnoses" (2019). Human beings are simply not image analysis machines. We're subject to fatigue, bias, and other influences beyond what's in the slides at hand. A human can only train their mental discernment "algorithm" on thousands of example images before they start making potentially life-or-death decisions at work.

Corporate greed has taken a stranglehold in many medical institutions. That makes it exceedingly challenging for the boots on the ground—such as nurses and technicians—to provide quality care. Managerial bonuses and promotions are predicated on a department's bottom-line financial performance rather than on aggregate patient wellness. Many times, Catherine had to squeeze what should have been an hour-long counseling session into a ten-minute data dump in order to accommodate aggressive patient scheduling.

Topol acknowledges that "clinicians are squeezed for maximal productivity and profits. We spend less and less time with patients, and that time is compromised without human-to-human bonding" (2019). When patients don't get the facetime they need with their providers, they're left feeling harried, with incomplete information, and less likely to experience optimal health outcomes.

Burnout robs institutions of their best care providers, and sometimes even totally removes those providers from the field. Clinicians want to do everything they can for those under their care. That drive to heal others' afflictions carried them through years of challenging and usually costly medical training. When that healer's employer can't give them what they need to do what they've been trained to do, they experience a grating cognitive dissonance. In a vicious cycle, "burnout leads to medical errors, and medical errors in turn promote burnout" (Topol 2019). Burnout can come from any one of a number of vectors, such as an overwhelming scope of responsibilities, a demanding schedule, inadequate compensation, or overexposure to traumatic scenarios—as in the ventilator shortages and general horror of the 2020 COVID pandemic.

Unnecessary testing poses yet another expensive problem in medicine. More testing isn't always better. Part of a genetic counselor's job, for example, is actually to determine how little genetic testing you can get away with while still collecting the hereditary information you need for critical decisions. Testing takes time and money while sometimes carrying its own risks. In the case of radiology, imaging usually comes with exposure to, well, radiation. It's not usually a terribly risky dose (depending on the type of scan), especially weighed against the potential of a missed cancer diagnosis. It's multi-factorial with nuances around variables like age and which regions you're scanning.

Regardless, no amount of radiation is completely without risk, so it's worth minimizing, within reason. That's not reflected in our health care system today. "For every one hundred Medicare recipients age sixty-five or older, each year there are more than fifty CT scans, fifty ultrasounds, fifteen MRIs, and ten PET scans. It's estimated that 30 to 50 percent of the eighty million CT scans in the United States are unnecessary" (Topol 2019). That has to change if we hope to make room for high-quality, targeted care.

Luddites, for our purposes, are those who resist the adoption of new technologies just because they are unfamiliar. Luddites hurt health care organizations and their patients. While healthy discernment and skepticism around novel tools and methods are critical, the failure to use them once they're proven effective can lead to massive opportunity costs. For example, "whole slide imaging (WSI) enables a physician to view an entire tissue sample on a slide, eliminating the need to have a microscope camera attachment. Pathologists have been slower than expected to adopt WSI and other digital techniques, which in turn has slowed the encroachment of AI into pathology" (Topol 2019).

Are pathologists exhibiting thoughtful conservativism about embracing technologies like WSI, or are they clinging to antiquated techniques because that's what's comfortable? Do doctors hope to prolong the relevance of their training by keeping newer, more sophisticated technology out of the clinic? Provided adequate continuing education programs, clinicians of all ages should have no reason to fear the latest and greatest.

THE PROMISE OF CLINICAL COMPUTER VISION

What role will computer vision play in remediating our health care system's maladies?

GIVE BACK TIME (FOR EMPATHY)

Computer vision will automate some of the tedious work that clinicians have, historically, had to do by hand.

The more time patients get to spend interfacing directly with the experts in charge of their care, the less likely they are to be hospitalized. One study, replicated successfully by Kaiser Permanente and Vanderbilt University Hospital, found that in more than two thousand subjects, "strengthening the relationship between patients and their doctors can decrease medical costs and improve patient health" in quantifiable ways (Tingley 2018). Patients who received inpatient and outpatient care from the same doctor had "20 percent fewer hospitalizations than their control-group counterparts." Building those relationships, however, takes work and time. Computer vision powered tools can replenish some of that time.

Seven years ago, one noted radiologist predicted that "within ten years no medical imaging study will be reviewed by a radiologist until it has been pre-analyzed by a machine" (Bryan 2016). That prediction wasn't terribly far off the mark, considering how quickly the field has since advanced. Merely two years after his prediction, a cross-disciplinary team at the University College London and DeepMind used computer vision "to markedly accelerate the segmentation processing of scans, achieving similar performance to experienced radiation oncologists for patients with head and neck cancer with remarkable time savings" (Topol 2019). Medical vision models are only getting faster and more accurate by the day. If Bryan's projection about automation by 2026 proves overly optimistic, it's because of the regulatory red tape, not the tech.

Computer vision's medical applications aren't limited to segmenting CT scans of the head and neck. An image-based "FDA-approved...algorithm called Deep Ventricle enables rapid analysis of the heart's blood flow, reducing a task that can take an hour as blood is drawn and measured by hand to a fifteen-second scan" (Topol 2019). Innovators and entrepreneurs ought to wonder: Which other medical processes can go *more than two hundred times faster* if automated with computer vision?

Clinicians should be less afraid that AI will steal their jobs and more excited at the prospect of shifting their focus back toward the human element. Topol mentions doctors Michael Recht and Nick Bryan, who believe "that machine learning and AI will enhance both the value and the professional satisfaction of radiologists by allowing us to spend more time performing functions that add value and influence patient care and less time doing rote tasks that we neither enjoy nor perform as well as machines" (2017). The same general principle holds true in most if not all domains.

MORE ACCURATE DIAGNOSES

Medical computer vision systems will do more than just save clinicians' time. These tools will raise fewer false alarms, saving patients from unnecessary distress and more expensive (and potentially invasive) diagnostics. They'll also miss fewer positive cases, saving lives with more reliable detection.

Radiologists, dermatologists, and pathologists all stand to offload chunks of their work to computer vision, which can actually outperform humans on a growing swath of tasks. These are just a few medical disciplines where visual pattern-recognition is particularly central. Computer vision can be applied to essentially any medical imaging technique with a large enough body of labeled training data—from x-rays to PET scans in two or three dimensions (or four, if you count time, as in the aforementioned blood flow analyzer).

As in self-driving, we're reaching a point where the only computer vision systems worth talking about are ones that perform at least as accurately as humans in their respective assignments. You'll begin to notice increasingly common instances of superhuman accuracy in medical image classifiers: "Radboud University in the Netherlands found that a deep neural network trained on more than 1,400 digital mammograms gave similarly accurate readings as those performed by twenty-three radiologists" (Topol 2019).

Averaging the evaluations of many professionals is better than taking just one leading expert's opinion. That's why we seek second or third opinions before we subject ourselves to risky surgeries or other dramatic courses of treatment, even when we basically trust our primary doctor. Now that visual analysis algorithms have started demonstrably outperforming *teams* of experts, it's high time to pave the regulatory path to roll these tools into the fabric of our health care workflows and infrastructure.

Many more critical diagnosis tasks are ripe for the transition to (at least partial) automation. For example, "in another study of pathology slides by researchers from New York University, the algorithmic accuracy for diagnosing subtypes of lung cancer was quite impressive (AUC = 0.97); half of the slides had been misclassified by pathologists" (Topol 2019).

AUC is a general performance indicator for predictive models; those with an AUC closer to one than zero are basically better. In this example, the machines clearly won out, but once again, pathologists have no reason to fear for their jobs. The synthesis of machine pattern recognition and human contextual judgment is really where it's at. "The Computer Science and AI Laboratory (CSAIL) group at MIT developed a...deep network for diagnosis of cancer metastasis to lymph nodes with four hundred whole slide images. The algorithm markedly reduced the pathologist error rate, but interestingly combining the pathologist and machine reading was clearly the best, with almost no errors" (Topol 2019).

What's astonishing about this is that four hundred samples is a pittance when it comes to training datasets for deep learning. What if we made more high-quality training data available for research projects like these? For now, there's comfort in knowing that the machines can still benefit from our help here and there.

Bear in mind that looking at a closed system's raw performance metrics doesn't give us the whole story. A skin cancer classification algorithm outperformed more than twenty Stanford dermatologists on sets of photographic and dermoscopic images, but Topol rightly points out that "an algorithmic test drive is not the same as using a technology in the real world. To date, very few patients of non-European ancestry have been included in algorithmic training" (2019). Should medical professionals deploy an automated image analysis system if it's only effective for certain skin colors? We'll touch on ethical considerations like these in a subsequent section.

SPOT HIDDEN PATTERNS

Computer vision is capable of detecting patterns in images that are impossible to detect with the naked eye—even highly trained naked eyes. Topol reports that "the texture of brain MRI images could predict a particular genomic anomaly...that's relevant to surviving certain types of brain cancer" (2019). That was impossible before we applied machine learning to medical images.

Furthermore, Topol notes that "using deep learning algorithms to read MRI scans of patients with colon cancer could reveal whether a patient has a critical tumor-gene mutation, known as KRAS, awareness of which should significantly influence treatment decisions" (2019). Those with cancerous genetic predispositions tend to live longer and happier lives the sooner they find out about those predispositions, so it's important for us to have more than one way to identify them. Traditionally we've only used genetic sequencing (of saliva, blood, or skin-punch biopsies) to gain knowledge of such mutations.

CHEAPER, SAFER TECHNIQUES BECOME MORE EFFECTIVE

We can lower medical expenses and expose ourselves to smaller doses of radiation by enhancing simpler imaging techniques with computer vision analysis.

Just by living day-to-day life, the average person is naturally exposed to some trivial amount of "background" radiation, to the tune of about three mSv (millisieverts) per year, at least in the United States (American Cancer Society 2018). One mammogram "exposes a woman to 0.4 mSv, or about the amount a person would expect to get from natural background exposure over seven weeks." That's a perfectly reasonable price to pay, given the importance of early breast cancer detection. Patients who require a PET/CT scan, however, are exposed "to about twenty-five mSv of radiation. This is equal to about eight years of average background radiation exposure." That's a considerable risk to incur, so doctors must have very good reason to order such costly testing. What if we could extract more information from simpler scans?

It turns out that we can. "Applying deep learning to X-ray images of hip fractures can lead to diagnoses as accurate as those derived from the more advanced—and so more expensive—image techniques, including MRI, nuclear bone scans, or CT, which doctors otherwise turn to when analyses of X-rays give uncertain results" (Topol 2019). The hip hardly seems like the only area that could benefit from this sort of post-processing approach. I'd much rather make the computational machinery work harder, by processing high-resolution image data, than subject myself to any more radiation than necessary.

AUTOMATE TIME-CONSUMING TASKS

Remember autonomous vehicle engineer Paul Filitchkin, the newish father? He alerted me to the existence of computer-vision-based lifeguard systems. Evidently, many toddlers drown every year in seemingly innocuous bodies of water like backyard pools. Now a slew of systems on the market (such as SwimEye, Poseidon, and AngelEye) use computer vision to continuously monitor such bodies of water, sounding the alarm when they detect anything closely resembling a drowning humanoid.

Computer vision can be used for this kind of monitoring task to free up hands in the clinic as well. "Surveillance videos of patients could help determine whether there is risk of a patient pulling out their endotracheal (breathing) tube and other parameters not captured by vital signs, reducing the burden on the nurse for detection. The ICU Intervene DNN, from MIT's CSAIL, helps doctors predict when a patient will need mechanical ventilation or vasopressors and fluid boluses to support blood pressure, along with other interventions" (Topol 2019). Nurses have enough work to do already; they don't need the additional burden of continuously monitoring already partly automated systems.

ADVANCE BIOLOGICAL RESEARCH

Preventive medicine is obviously preferable to hospitalization, but even more fundamentally, we have to keep expanding our scientific horizons to more fully understand the human body. Along with deep space and the bottom of the sea, parts of our own biology remain enshrouded in mystery, especially surrounding the brain. Improved image analysis tools help us reach new depths of understanding, which informs the next generation of downstream clinical applications.

When biologists can trust automated systems to handle tedious frequency measurements and microscopic classification work, it broadens their horizons to more interesting and novel questions. Wet lab work is infamously tedious. Google and Harvard collaborated to make it less so by developing "open-source algorithms that can accurately predict how samples would fluoresce without the need for any fluorescent preparation" (Topol 2019). That will save overqualified postdoctoral researchers some pipetting work, plus open the door to entirely new avenues of study. Historically, we've used fluorescence microscopy to enhance the visibility of specific cellular elements—at the cost of damaging the very cells under investigation. Longer-term studies would be impossible without computer vision.

How did the researchers achieve the ability to simulate fluorescence without the need to actually fluoresce the cells? "They trained the DNN [deep neural network] by matching fluorescent labeled images with unlabeled ones, repeating the process millions of times. This method, known as in silico labeling as well as augmented microscopy was called 'a new epoch in cell biology'" (Topol 2019). Faced with a dearth of labeled training data, it's possible to use a weakly trained vision model to *automatically label* unlabeled image data, synthetically expanding the training set and quality checking as you go. We can expect to hear about more instances where "in silico" techniques replace or augment "in vitro" (Latin for "in glass") methods.

SIDE EFFECTS

As with many medicines, computer vision solutions come with some potential negative side effects. I would be remiss not to mention some of those roadblocks and unintended consequences here.

OVERBLOWN HYPE

On the opposite end of the spectrum from Luddites, we have those who are *too* eager to adopt some attractive new technology, even though its marketing campaigns are more successful than its clinical trials. Topol acknowledges that "some pronouncements could be considered exuberant...such as Andrew Ng's suggestion that radiologists might be easier to replace than their executive assistants." Medicine is a high-stakes domain where regulatory hurdles exist for a reason. It's exciting that technology is unlocking all of this wonderful potential, but we can't let that hype bypass our institutional safeguards. The gatekeepers are right to be at least somewhat skeptical, for reasons delineated below.

SILOED DATA

Patients and organizations hold their medical data close to the chest, and data is the lifeblood of machine learning algorithms. Understandably, folks aren't as forthcoming with their health data as they are with their employment status or consumer habits; that's been codified into federal law. The Health Insurance Portability and Accountability Act of 1996 (HIPAA) is meant to "protect sensitive patient health information from being disclosed without the patient's consent or knowledge" while allowing enough information flow for quality health care (CDC 2022).

While I'm grateful that my medical information is safe, I also recognize that this is part of the reason some of the best and brightest data scientists are drawn to fields with less red tape. It's easier to find (or create) an open-source image classification dataset of cats and dogs than it is to find labeled three-dimensional scans of the heart or lungs. It's easier for me to query an open web database (about, say, urban trees) than it is to figure out how to gain access to anonymized patient data from my local hospital and combine that with even more (probably messy) data from other hospitals.

The challenge of collecting sufficient data to train highly performant computer vision models is formidable in medicine.

NARROW APPLICATIONS

The medical applications discussed here are a far cry from the dystopian incarnations of general artificial intelligence you've seen in sci-fi movies like HAL 9000 from Kubrick's *2001: A Space Odyssey*. A "narrow" image classification model, trained purely to determine whether or not moles are cancerous, is never going to start teaching itself Latin and flirting with other AI apps. Topol quotes "Gregory Moore, VP of health care at Google and himself a radiologist, [who] has observed that 'there literally have to be thousands of algorithms to even come close to replicating what a radiologist can do on a given day'" (2019). This means we still have loads of work to do and market opportunities to explore in medicine for AI practitioners, provided they have the patience to acquire the requisite training data. Specific small problems (and their subproblems) require specific solutions. The good news is that thousands of machine learning practitioners are looking for work of this nature today.

CLINICAL JOB DISPLACEMENT

Until recently, the workers with the most automatable jobs tended to be the same ones least equipped to make radical career changes—like starting from scratch in a new type of job or investing in continued education. Now, even highly trained and credentialed health care experts have to wonder which parts of their skillsets will remain marketable in the coming decade. Topol thinks "a bigger challenge than finding new jobs for displaced workers…may be creating new jobs that are not better or, largely, performed by a machine" (2019). Where is the motivation for a cost-minded employer to make an expensive job opening when some software service can adequately tick most of the same boxes? My personal forecast is that as medical technology advances, a larger fraction of clinical jobs will involve participating in the automation of one's very own specialized job responsibilities.

ALGORITHMIC TRUST ISSUES

Last but not least, there are reasons not to implicitly trust the technology—even when the performance metrics look good.

MULTIPLYING BIAS/INEQUITY

Deep Medicine gives a nod to Cathy O'Neil's *Weapons of Math Destruction.* My opinion is that anybody working anywhere near AI should be required to read O'Neil's book at least once; it gets very short shrift here. Topol echoes O'Neil's central argument, that algorithmic bias "pervasively affects perceptions of gender, race, ethnicity, socioeconomic class, and sexual orientation. The impact can be profound, including who gets a job, or even a job interview, how professionals get ranked," and so forth (2019). How might such hairy ethical considerations as these manifest in medical computer vision?

One Stanford professor attempted to demonstrate a "gaydar" (sexual orientation classifier) built with computer vision. The preprint he and his research partner published bore the title "Deep neural networks are more accurate than humans at detecting sexual orientation from facial images" (Wang and Kosinski 2018). It was sensational because on paper the model appeared to outperform humans at guessing sexual orientations given nothing but images. The paper and the ensuing news coverage furrowed many eyebrows and rankled the LGBTQ+ community. Hadn't we established that physiognomy, or divination based on facial features, is squarely in the realm of pseudoscience?

Notably, of the 35,000 images in the model's final training set, "all were white, the researchers said, because they could not find enough dating profiles of gay minorities to generate a statistically valid result" (Murphy 2017). That's a significant omission for a model claiming better-than-human performance on a task that probably shouldn't be whimsically undertaken in the first place. Some projects are better abandoned during the ideation phase.

A refutation to this controversial paper from the leader of Google's AI group in Seattle demonstrated "how the obvious differences between lesbian or gay and straight faces in selfies relate to grooming, presentation, and lifestyle—that is, differences in culture, not in facial structure" (Arcas et al. 2018). In other words, the vision model was probably not relying primarily on facial features like jaw structure or eye shape to predict sexual orientation. It was learning mainly from wardrobe and hairstyle choices, eyewear, makeup, and other externalities. It was sloppy data science at best.

It is possible to build similarly "high-scoring" machine learning models that are intrinsically harmful, even in medicine.

Topol writes that "in health care, there's even the potential to deliberately build algorithms that are unethical, such as basing prediction of patient care recommendations on insurance or income status" (2019). It's not always obvious when supposedly protected data like income status leaks from one column into another. Even patient zip codes can become a proxy for income status. If many high-net-worth individuals live in one zip code, and very few live in another, feeding a "zip code" column into a machine learning model, which predicts, for example, a patient's likelihood to pay down large medical bills on time, is likely to result in unfair biases stacked against folks in the low-income zip code. In computer vision applications, bias might look more like a skin cancer detector that only works well on light-skinned folks—perhaps because it's more challenging to collect image samples and train a quantitatively "impressive" vision model across a wide variety of skin tones.

UNDERPERFORMANCE

Making money and getting published can become perverse incentives. A so-called researcher with no scruples can cobble together a model that doesn't do nearly as well in the wild as it does in a controlled environment and then shill that as a product.

Topol quotes a radiologist with AI expertise, who wrote that "any PhD can train a deep learning network to classify images with apparent human-level performance on cross-validation. Take it into the real world and they will all underperform"

(2019). Cross-validation is essentially a model training and evaluation technique that's supposed to mitigate this very problem, helping predictive models generalize beyond the data they're trained on, but it's not sufficient on its own. To be truly rigorous, cross-validation should not be the final step in a model's benchmarking. A separate "test" subset of the initially available data should be carefully reserved for a strictly one-time final evaluation, once the model has been optimized using cross-validation. Only then can you really have some idea of how well your model is performing.

Technical jargon aside, researchers and entrepreneurs in the medical space should do their best to be honest with themselves and their potential customers. The results matter. A system's true performance will show sooner or later.

MULTIPLIED LIABILITY

Medicine is one domain where it's clear that most decisions are too important to leave completely up to the machines, at least for now. At the end of the day, "doctors, hospitals, and health systems would be held accountable for decisions that machines might make, even if the algorithms used were rigorously tested and considered fully validated" (Topol 2019). The patient's family doesn't care whether a dermatologist or an expensive piece of software failed to spot grandpa's cancerous mole; the summons ends up in the same mailbox. Malpractice insurance only goes so far, and doctors aren't eager to test those limits.

O'Neil underscores how machine learning algorithms, and blind trust in them, can take regular human mistakes and multiply them at devastating scale. Imagine a machine learning system that "recommends the wrong dose of insulin. If a human made this mistake, it could lead to a hypoglycemic coma or death in one patient. If an AI system made the error, it could injure or kill hundreds or even thousands" (Topol 2019). The same goes for coronary blood flow analysis scanners, or lung cancer classification systems. You don't want to release buggy firmware updates over Wi-Fi when that could put everyone in possession of your device at direct risk of lawsuits or death. Tesla Inc. comes to mind here for no particular reason.

FALLING OUT OF DATE

Even if a computer vision model were hypothetically perfect at the time of its genesis, it could not stay perfect forever. A data training set (say, of medical images) only reflects the world and its patients as it is, not necessarily as it shall become. For example, there will always be some minuscule drift in the output of aging radiological imaging devices, which software or hardware engineers will need to compensate for over time. Human biology itself may shift in some small, unexpected way.

ALGORITHMIC OPACITY

In most deep learning-based systems today:

> The creators of the algorithm can't explain how [the predictions] happened. The same phenomenon comes up in medical AI. One example is the capacity for deep learning to match the diagnostic capacities of a team of twenty-one board-certified dermatologists in classifying skin lesions as cancerous or benign. The Stanford

computer science creators of that algorithm still don't
know exactly what features account for its success
(Topol 2019).

Deep learning models are notoriously opaque "black-box" systems, where it's mathematically impossible to know exactly how the algorithm arrives at the decisions it makes. We know what data we're feeding in, and we can draw "saliency maps" to gain some insight into which regions of an image are particularly important to a vision model, but it won't come out and tell us exactly *why*. In an upcoming chapter, we hear from a postdoctoral researcher at MIT's AI lab who is pushing AI transparency, which in the case of deep learning, starts with smaller, simpler models that are more easily interpretable. That's especially important in high-liability domains like medicine, where errors must be traceable to some root cause.

DISCHARGE

If I'm reading Topol correctly, machines are starting to beat humans at an increasing number of very specific clerical and diagnostic tasks in the clinic. That number is likely to keep growing. As these tasks begin to overlap and ratchet up in responsibility, whole human jobs will start to change or vanish. Thanks to computer vision, radiologists, pathologists, dermatologists, and other experts who deal with the interpretation of visual patterns will find that they have the capacity to either handle more patients, lining their employer's pockets, or increase the quality of care they provide to the patients they already serve. Given the squalid state of American health care today, let's hope we gravitate toward the latter.

Topol rings splendidly true to me when he writes that "emotional intelligence needs to take precedence in the selection of future doctors over qualities that are going to be of progressively diminished utility." He says, "the fundamentals—empathy, presence, listening, communication, the laying of hands, and the physical exam—are the building blocks for a cherished relationship between patient and doctor" (Topol 2019). I can anecdotally confirm this, as someone who recently switched primary care providers to a doctor who actually looks me in the eye rather than remaining totally fixated on their computer monitor. I've never been more satisfied with any of my personal medical decisions.

05

YOUR OWN WORST CRITIC

Jason Antic's home energy bill is probably considerably higher than yours. In fact, he said he's "basically maxing out what you can do in a house before you burn your house down. And even then, I wouldn't let it run while I'm gone."

Today, Jason owns and operates his own small but successful (and somewhat energy-thirsty) computer vision business from home. Back when he was a starry-eyed teenager, he aspired to create video games. That aspiration led him into a conventional programming career. What started as a dream to make thrilling, interactive digital experiences became a cubicle job in the vibrant and life-affirming world of insurance technology.

He says it was "basically Initech, you know, like from *Office Space*. I did that for like a decade until I finally figured out it was pretty much going nowhere." Jason's long hair and San Diego home base don't scream cubicle tech drone. I'm glad he found a way out.

In the mid-2010s, Jason sensed a marked acceleration in AI research. He says he "probably read about it on Reddit." He saw this wave of advancement as an avenue to a new and more colorful career. I can relate. In 2017, I was burned out at my night-shift role in a film and TV post-production studio. Like Jason, I left a job I couldn't stomach any longer to go learn everything I could about AI and how it could be applied in creative and helpful new ways. After a decade of grinding nine-to-five in insurance, Jason needed a clean break, a window of time to drill into his intellectual curiosities and build something completely new, something of his own, from scratch.

He was particularly drawn to computer vision. I asked most folks I interviewed for this book to define computer vision in their own words, as concisely as possible, and I particularly enjoy Jason's definition:

> Giving the computer the ability to identify objects and scenes in a photo or video in order to be able to classify it or...identify what's in the picture and to manipulate it, potentially. It's a very broad range of things. It's basically, even more simply, *like giving eyes to software.* That's something we didn't have ten years ago. Practically, it's a new skill. *It's a new sense for your computer.*

Computer vision lets computers do more than just "see," however. In a manner of speaking, you could say it allows computers to *dream* in images as well.

Until recently, CV applications largely just extracted information from images, such as bucketing whole images into categories like "cat" or "dog." They may have gone another step, segmenting images into discrete parts and then labeling those separate parts as discrete objects. For example, facial recognition algorithms locate regions of images containing faces and then attempt to label those faces with human identities. Now, however, a massive groundswell in research is focused on automatically generating *new* imagery—seemingly from nothing. These *generative models* have flooded the mainstream, and like so many elements of the AI landscape, their explosive potential is simultaneously magnificent and terrifying.

Suffice it to say that Jason caught wind of generative AI during its nascence, well before it slipped into the limelight.

He immersed himself in FastAI, a free online course on deep learning created by industry thought leaders Jeremy Howard and Rachel Thomas. He said he "decided to do a capstone project to solidify my understanding of the material because I really think you should...not just do toy examples but really torture yourself with an actual problem." I've heard this refrain countless times from numerous sources—particularly on the quest to learn to code but also regarding learning in general. Reading theory is fine and good, but the stickiest, most rewarding knowledge comes from stumbling one's way toward some concrete, practical goal. That was the case for Jason and his computer vision project.

Where did the project idea come from? Jason told me that over "the course of the summer, I was just writing down ideas that popped up, mostly when I took a walk. And one of the twenty-some ideas I had for a capstone project was colorization." In the FastAI course, Jason says he learned "about these things that were just coming up called GANs: generative adversarial networks. They were pretty limited at the time in their application...but I had this idea that you could use it to make colorization more...colorful." Historically, if you wanted to colorize a black-and-white image (for example, a portrait of your veteran great-grandfather in uniform), you had to hire an artist, like the Brazilian contemporary Marina Amaral.

Colorization gives new life to black-and-white images. Monochrome photos can often feel too antiquated to strike the same sentimental impact as their color counterparts. Regarding her project "Faces of Auschwitz," Amaral said she sought to "give people the opportunity to connect to the victims on an emotional level, in a way that is perhaps impossible to do if you see them in black and white, representing something old, a historical event that took place so many years ago" (Mallonee 2018). The first time I saw copies of the rare color photographs of Dr. Martin Luther King Jr., it made the events of his life feel more recent and visceral to me. Colorization is just one of countless image-based tasks we can hope to partially automate with AI, but it's a valuable endeavor.

Digital styluses and modern illustration software have accelerated manual colorization to some extent, but it's still painstaking, skilled labor. Black-and-white images contain loads of ambiguity: Grass could be green or brown, the sky could be blue or purple, and bricks could be red or yellow. Experienced artists like Amaral conduct meticulous research to discern the historically correct colors for minuscule details, such as for specific decorations on military uniforms. Otherwise, saturating a fully desaturated image can involve making a good many contextual assumptions.

Automatic colorization algorithms existed long before Jason's, which he dubbed "DeOldify," but they were primitive. The results were disappointingly bland and unrealistic, especially compared to the work of a skilled artisan like Amaral. DeOldify has helped change that. Jason maintains that no colorization algorithm comes close to the mastery of an artist like Amaral, but DeOldify certainly improved upon what was available in the software division. What started as Jason's class project ultimately brought him Twitter fame, a licensing deal with MyHeritage (a genealogy platform), and a new career—growing his own computer vision powered business from home.

But what is a GAN? I asked Jason to explain DeOldify's underlying mechanism in lay terms. He said a GAN typically uses:

> Two AI's: One is the thing that actually makes the colorization, and then another, which is your "art critic," saying whether or not it looks realistic. The art critic starts out kind of...really bad. He doesn't know what he's doing. And the colorizer starts out really bad. But they keep going back and forth, giving each other feedback. The colorizer keeps making gradually better colorizations, and the critic has to up their game, figuring out what's a good colorization and what's not. They just keep doing this, back and forth, until they arrive at a point where you actually have good colorization.

While most of DeOldify is open source, some of the more advanced features and latest upgrades are reserved for the version Jason and his business partner license to MyHeritage. "We were very glad to have MyHeritage to license the technology to because then we didn't have to worry about budgeting for servers, building the app, monetizing it, dealing with angry customers, stuff like that." As of this writing, users have access to Jason's work through the MyHeritage app.

Simply upload your old black-and-white photos, push a button, and MyHeritage colorizes them with DeOldify's algorithmic (partly) secret sauce.

Is there room for more such solopreneurship powered by computer vision, or are advances in the field just pulling us closer to a dystopia of disinformation and distraction?

The story of DeOldify demonstrates that working at a giant, evil tech mega-corp isn't the only way to make a living in AI. Under the right circumstances (like having a supportive partner), a sufficiently motivated engineer can leverage their creativity to adapt freely available resources to make a living on their own terms. We're bound to discover more healthy and productive use cases for computer vision that can, for example, bring a historical moment out of greyscale and into vibrant living color at the push of a button. Nonetheless, while Jason has experienced harmless success building his own business around machine learning, he's still wary of its potential for evil, which we'll cover in later chapters.

The world of generative art is evolving so rapidly that even since I began research for this book, GANs have lost their crown as the state of the art in image generation methodologies. Researchers at leading AI lab OpenAI demonstrated that "a different deep learning architecture, called *diffusion models*, addresses...shortcomings of GANs. They show that not only are diffusion models better at capturing a greater breadth of the training data's variance compared to GANs, but they also beat the SOTA [state-of-the-art] GANs in image generation tasks" (Fawaz 2021). In other words, this new wave of models is not only easier to develop, but they also produce more convincing and lifelike image outputs—faster. By the time you read this, we will have probably already moved on to the next generation of performant generative art architectures.

Regardless of the engine under the hood, a fundamental shift is underway. Software tools that can paint uncannily realistic "new" images have arrived, and they've very recently become convincing enough to begin shaking the social fabric. Beyond colorizing black-and-white images, today's state-of-the-art generative image models can upscale lower-resolution images, paint out stragglers in your engagement photos, or design your brand's new logo based on a text description. This opens entirely new creative landscapes to artists and others interested in dabbling with software tools built around generative algorithms. We'll begin to see more generative capabilities featured by default in smartphones and other consumer devices.

These new capabilities deeply concern those who make their living creating visual works. Will generative models put them out of a job? Vice reported on a canvas print, which "came in first at the Colorado State Fair's fine art competition using an AI generated artwork"; the headline didn't fail to mention that "artists are pissed" about it (Gault 2022). AI enthusiast Jason Allen created the piece for the digital art category, using a program that required no human talent other than the ability to experiment with various text prompts and select favorable outputs. He applied some minimal post-processing, but this moment still marked a new paradigm for visual art creation. Tempers flare over whether creating this way is fraudulent or futuristic.

Even if you think about a generative algorithm as just another brush in the artist's toolbox, questions about attribution remain. Generative models are necessarily trained on enormous swaths of existing digital media, often without permission from the works' original artists. Sample images are programmatically "scraped" (downloaded en masse) from image-sharing websites and thrown into the model's training set. Only after an initial salvo of backlash are artists being offered any option to exclude their works from new generative model training sets. Inclusion is still typically the default—as is the case with so many facial recognition databases. If you download and run a pretrained diffusion model today, you can even go so far as to prompt it for images "in the style of [some famous living artist's name]"—and US copyright law still has nothing to protect visual styles. This sets the stage for legal battles that could extend well into the next decade as we grapple once again with fundamental questions around the nature of art and its patronage.

Not that they're the arbiters of good and evil, but "venture capitalists have increased investment in Generative AI by 425 percent since 2020 to $2.1 billion," in a show of confidence that at least a few great business ideas are waiting to be mined from the space (Pennington 2023). That's fertile ground for the next round of AI art entrepreneurs as long as they're willing to weather the brewing regulatory storm. The tools are becoming so accessible now that many probably won't need venture capital money to get their generative art companies off the ground, if Antic's tale is any indication. Let's just be sure to squash the apps that undress people without their consent.

06

AN EYE FOR TALENT

Somewhere in Hollywood, a Disney computer vision system studies audience facial reactions to as-yet unreleased movies.

Francis Ford Coppola, the director of the revered *Godfather* trilogy, also happens to be the godfather of movie test screenings. While editing *Apocalypse Now* in 1978, Coppola says he held advance screenings where "filmgoers were given a letter...inviting them 'to help me finalize the film'" (Phillips 2005).

Such test screenings hadn't been established as standard practice in Hollywood, but Coppola's background was actually in theater. He said, "Reviewing theater work is part of a longstanding tradition, and I was looking for a modern way of accomplishing it" (Willens 2000). He took from one medium to inform the other, forever changing the way filmmakers approach the editing process.

Coppola was essentially data mining. He hoped to quantify his work on several subjective axes in order to inform some final creative decisions. He wanted honest opinions on whether or not to include certain scenes or to augment particular musical selections and narration. As his test audience watched the rough cut, he turned to watch them.

It's not like Coppola was the very first filmmaker to ever run a test screening. "Frank Capra, Alfred Hitchcock and other greats liked to have their films shown to preview audiences," to take notes on laughter levels and bathroom capacity as their films progressed (Willens 2000). Coppola spearheaded the formalization of this process, priming the audience with prompts before the screening and conducting written exit surveys. Future generations of directors took note.

Test screenings persist as a common tool for filmmakers and studios in Hollywood, nearly five decades after *Apocalypse Now*. Not all filmmakers universally adore them, however. Studios can abuse test screenings to round the gritty edges off of what's intended to be edgy work. Mechanisms like these inherently make big studio movies more milquetoast, slightly more paint-by-numbers, but I digress. Many filmmakers still want to know which parts of their films drag and which punchlines or jump-scares garner the most chuckles and screams. Almost every major film with enough time in their schedule conducts test screenings toward the end of the editing process.

The problem is that there's still no perfect way to measure movie audience reactions. Caltech's Dr. Yisong Yue noticed two primary methods studios use to evaluate movies today: conducting surveys, just like Coppola in the seventies, or sticking sensors on audience members. Sensors can measure variables like heart rate and skin conductivity, i.e., sweat response—an okay proxy metric for fear. Dr. Yue said:

The drawback of the former [surveys] is that it happens after the movie is over. So you're still trying to remember what you were feeling as you were watching the movie. The drawback of the latter [sensors] is that it's actually disruptive to the movie watching experience, right? Things are on your skin, for example. And so those different technologies are either unreliable or cannot scale (Yue and Houghton 2017).

That's where computer vision enters the fold. In collaboration with Disney research in 2017, Dr. Yue and his team repurposed infrared cameras and open-source tools to create "a new deep-learning software capable of assessing complex audience reactions to movies using the viewer's facial expressions" (Perkins 2017). It leverages the best of both worlds, analyzing audience reactions to movies in real time before they forget what they saw—without invasive sensors to remove them from the viewing experience. Now computer vision plays a role in supercharging contemporary entertainment.

We're doing what a lot of directors want to do anyways, watch the audience's reactions as they're watching your pilot showing of a film for the first time. But we're building a computational tool to basically empower directors to be able to scale up their analysis (Yue and Houghton 2017).

Directors and producers could leverage automated test screenings to simultaneously evaluate different version of the same film. If they're undecided on version A or version B of a particular scene, they could simply show fifty audiences version A, show the other fifty version B, and measure which version got more laughs on aggregate. Several such variations could be interspersed to quickly unearth the ideal version of a film, previously buried in the unfinished edit.

It's important to remember that this is one of many *narrow* applications of AI, meaning it won't be able to perform other tasks, even similar ones, without very deliberate tweaks. Dr. Yue said, "The movie theater setting is a great first step, because in many ways, it's a controlled environment; people are sitting down, they're watching a movie, and that's all they're doing" (2017). However, it's not out of the question that similar technologies could have applications outside of Hollywood.

Eric Topol talks about computer vision systems for monitoring hospital patients on ventilators. Dr. Yue believes we could use improved monitoring systems for the elderly to improve safety at home in the absence of caregivers. Yue believes that "as machines become more embedded in our daily lives and provide assistance, many of them need to exhibit greater social and behavioral intelligence in order to properly gauge human response and react to it" (Yue and Houghton 2017). That's the broader problem he's hacking on.

BEYOND ROBO-TAXIES

In the previous chapter, we discussed how computer vision encompasses systems that not only extract high-level meaning from images but also generate new images—perhaps from a text description. While automating driving may be, to many, the most attractive and immediate computer vision engineering challenge today, and certain medical applications are contenders for the most noble, almost any industry where people use their eyes to perform some job function is now ripe for automation or algorithmic assistance. Here we'll explore some low-hanging fruit, with examples from image-centric domains like film production, sports broadcasting, and the consumer experience.

Thanks to the ongoing computer vision renaissance, creatives in visual media will have increasingly powerful tools at their disposal. Adobe, a software company best known for their popular photo and video editing programs, recognizes the value of deep-learning-powered computer vision tools to enhance and accelerate creative output. A feature available in both Photoshop and After Effects called "content-aware fill" enables users to "quickly remove unwanted objects like boom mics, logos, or even people" from still or moving images with just a few clicks (Adobe Inc. 2023). A product manager at Adobe told me that "when we did content-aware fill it came from looking at the PatchMatch paper, which...was very, very cool, and kind of wildly ambitious." The computer science graduate student who wrote that paper did so in 2010 after several internships at Adobe. It was revolutionary at the time, but more recently, the content-aware fill features have been retrofitted with a newer deep neural network-based image in-painting system. Now it's better than ever.

Another futuristic feature Adobe makes available to video editors is called the Morph Cut. Often when you're editing interviews, you must edit around undesirable discontinuities like "uhms," "ahs," and long pauses. Making hard cuts around those moments would look jarring to viewers, causing what's known as a "jump cut." Morph Cut was "designed to smooth out these cuts in order to make talking-head style interviews look seamless—sort of like what autotune does for audio. Morph Cut uses interpolation and face tracking to effectively fill in the gaps" (Savvides 2015). In a way, the Morph Cut is sort of like a miniature harmless deepfake, used just to eschew commonplace verbal flubs. This is computer vision at work, saving video editors from performing rote, tedious tasks so they may have more time to express themselves in creative new ways.

As someone who used to work in cinema post-production, I have ideas for how computer vision could be used to catalyze film editing workflows. For example, there is the perennial problem of audio synchronization. Often, audio and video tracks are recorded separately on the film set, and the metadata meant to help realign them goes awry or goes missing altogether. The film slate (or "clapper") makes a helpful ground truth in such cases. When the "sticks" are clapped, they create instantaneous, simultaneous auditory and visual signals. A loud clap blasts the sound team's microphones, and the camera registers the split-second change of state from "open" to "closed" sticks. Those clear signals are easy to spot in video and audio files downstream—or at least they should be.

From 2016 to 2018, I spent countless mind-numbing hours re-aligning audio and video files with the often-paltry help of the clapper's analog signals. That's what ultimately convinced me that I needed to find a way to learn to code.

In 2022, having learned to code, I designed a custom image dataset and used it to train an object detection model to recognize film slates in images. This surprisingly accurate model could be further developed into a push-button tool that any video editor could use to locate the instant of the slate clap in a video clip—just from the image without audio files. A niche market of folks sitting in dark Hollywood back rooms staring at images of film slates on computer screens might pay a lot for something like that.

GOOD EYE

The 2011 movie *Moneyball* underscored the importance of statistics in baseball, a field also known as "sabermetrics." At one time it was pioneering just to create composite metrics like "earned run average" or "WHIP" (walks plus hits per inning pitched). Now, computer vision is making inroads into baseball and other sports measurement, extracting and amalgamating data in novel ways. Doctoral candidate Connor Heaton at Penn State developed an entirely new and improved baseball player evaluation model, incorporating such rich and specific information as pitch type, launch angle, velocity, and rotation:

> "This work has the potential to significantly advance the state of the art in sabermetrics," said Prasenjit Mitra, professor of information sciences and technology and co-author on the paper. "To the best of our knowledge, ours is the first to capture and represent a nuanced state of the game and utilize this information as the context to evaluate the individual events that are counted by traditional statistics—for example, by automatically building a model that understands key moments and clutch events" (Hallman 2022).

Traditional sabermetrics leave much to be desired in the way of context-specific intel. Not only does Heaton and Mitra's paper use fine-grain data extracted from imaging devices as input, but it also borrows statistical techniques developed in the context of computer vision to more completely describe player behaviors (Heaton and Mitra 2022). In other words, pragmatic mathematical lessons, learned in the process of developing computer vision algorithms, can be applied outside of pure vision tasks—sort of like how dehydrated food developed for space exploration has become a wilderness backpacker favorite. Nuanced approaches like Heaton's will lead us into a new era of sports coaching.

Most sports have something to gain from computer-vision-powered analytics. For the aspiring soccer goalies, another paper (presented at the same MIT Sports Analytics Conference as Heaton's) described a working approach to harness "computer vision and machine learning models to appraise the save technique of professionals in a way those at lower levels can learn from" (Wear et al. 2022). The system extrapolates three-dimensional athlete pose data from regular two-dimensional broadcast footage to deconstruct how pro goalkeepers move and react in specific scenarios. With that, it establishes the best approaches to handle any given goalkeeping situation; human players can then use this to inform their training. It's clear that models analyzing player and ball (or puck, or bobsled, or whatever) movements will play an increasingly actionable role in sports coaching and strategy as the technology matures.

SUPER SMART SUPERMARKET

Consumers haven't had much reason to get excited about virtual and augmented reality technology until recently. In just the last decade, the companies designing such virtual reality experiences have taken us through iterations ranging from niche tinkerer fodder to fairly compelling mass market gaming devices. Even more recently, flagship chip manufacturers have reached an inflection point on chip performance and size where we're finally removing some of the major hardware limitations that have hampered VR and AR possibilities for decades. This bodes well for the future of wearable augmented-reality technology in the living room and out in the open world.

Historically, a passably high-quality virtual reality experience could only be rendered by, at minimum, a powerful gaming PC (with perhaps a water-cooling system and a powerful GPU, or several). VR headsets had to be tethered via a bulky bundle of cables to the PC, limiting the wearer's mobility and creating a trip hazard to manage. You may have also had to mount and calibrate various extra sensors around the room to track your movement and translate that movement back into the virtual world. It was not exactly a plug-and-play experience; some of the most graphically advanced units on the market today still require such an elaborate setup, and for some, it's worth it. For the rest of us, it's a bit much.

Thanks to increasingly fast and minuscule mobile processing chips, today we have more affordable consumer devices like the Oculus Quest 2, which requires no additional living room infrastructure. The headset guides you through establishing a sensible boundary of play, so you don't blindly run into your own furniture. The cameras onboard the headset track your movement through physical space as you spin and dance around within the confines of your pre-defined safe zone. The headset handles all of its own graphical processing on board. There are no cable tethers, and no need to set up sensors around the room. It's a comparatively seamless VR experience for the masses. While it's still a bit hokey on graphics, that will change as the hardware continues to shrink.

VR headsets have become a novel holiday gift, but in order to shape the future, this sort of technology will have to come with (many more of) us everywhere we go, like our smartphones already do. Augmented reality glasses hold the promise to superimpose elements of the digital realm over our physical reality, enhancing the physical world with web-connected constructs. They're just not good enough as of this writing. That should change in the next decade.

Google Glass was ahead of its time in 2013. The concept was futuristic, but the hardware was insufficient to impress the masses. It cost fifteen hundred dollars and came with a somewhat low-resolution video camera. Folks were justifiably worried that this spy-gadget-esque wearable might be the ultimate tool for privacy violation. Only eight thousand or so "explorers" were initially invited to beta test the hardware. Almost a decade later, Google Glass has taken refuge in limited enterprise use cases. For example, DHL straps these AR glasses on their warehouse workers to "scan items from racks before moving them into totes or bins on carts" hands-free, and "pickers now receive all picking instructions directly from Glass, right in their line of sight" (Google 2023). Glass customers include some household names like Volkswagen, General Electric, and Samsung, but I still can't personally say I know anyone using augmented reality glasses on a regular basis.

With AR in mind, I spoke to Tom Edwards about the future of computer vision's role in the consumer experience. Tom is a thought leader and marketing guru with his finger on the pulse of the tech world. He's continuously immersing himself in the primordial ooze of in-progress patent applications and industry publications to better forecast what the near future will look like. "Apple calls Tom 'bold and fearless,' Nintendo states, 'Tom has a level of expertise I've rarely seen in my career,' Hulu called Tom 'a leader in the digital realm,' Southwest Airlines states Tom 'is a forward thinker who pushes the convention,'" and he's the first person I've ever seen with more than one hundred glowing endorsements from former coworkers and clients on their LinkedIn profile (Edwards 2023). If nothing else, he's great at marketing himself.

Tom told me that generation Z "represents 40 percent of consumers, 96 percent of which game; 69 percent are used to using the camera as a platform. Eighty-three percent play with AR filters." He said that for gen Z, "the camera is basically a home screen." My friend's younger sibling, a zoomer, opened my eyes to the fact that those in the gen Z cohort frequently use social video platforms like TikTok to seek out information—in much the same way that I might Google something (as an aging millennial, stuck in my antiquated ways). These video-centric tendencies will come crashing into the physical world as soon as the computing hardware and wireless networks will support it. Tom believes that computer vision is:

> Going to be processing the real-world environment… to then render whatever digital overlays you're going to see in that real world. And to me, that's the real triggering moment where we'll see computer vision at scale. It's less about recognition and context and more

about activation, or enhancing the world around us,
and what we see based on our personal preferences.

Imagine you're visiting a friend who lives in Tokyo for the first time. On your way from the train station, you decide to stop for some groceries. You open your phone's map app to search for local supermarkets. You select one along your path with decent ratings. Your phone pipes turn-by-turn walking directions to your glasses, which superimpose semi-transparent guiding arrows and waypoints over the real physical world around you as you go. You arrive at the store.

The supermarket's whole inventory is kept meticulously up to date in a spatial database, which enables your glasses to guide you along the most optimal walking route to collect each of the items on your shopping list. This system doesn't care that your shopping list is in English, and the items are labeled in Japanese. When you direct your gaze to hold it over an item for a second, your glasses translate the Japanese label into English. Yup, that's mayonnaise. The store's algorithmic inventory management system offers you a discount on organic eggs as you approach them, hoping they'll be able to clear out some of their overstock while satisfying one of your grocery list items.

Have you ever stood gaping at a rack of five dozen spice jars at the supermarket, unable to quickly locate the smoked paprika? Computer vision and augmented reality could end such problems. Your AR glasses could draw boxes around items from your shopping list when it spots them on the shelf in real time. Tom is confident that we will see a paradigm shift away from "what we've seen to date, primarily using computer vision to extract information from large amounts of data, versus using that as a way to create and craft experiences that redefine our reality," and I tend to agree.

These are just a few of the ways in which computer vision will sculpt the future landscape of various industries. Those that lean heavily on optics and visual media, such as video and film production or sports broadcasting, will be first. The broader consumer experience will follow. Carpenters and architects will gain a new suite of tools. Oceanographers, pastry chefs, musicians, and aviators will be empowered, and so will you.

07

NEMATODE BRAINS

Technology often draws inspiration from nature, but Dr. Ramin Hasani went so far as to say (only half-jokingly) that "if you want to understand natural phenomena, I would say a machine learning system is also a natural phenomenon." How could that be remotely true, if the "A" in AI stands for "artificial," one of the textbook antonyms of "natural"?

Imagine an ever-expanding circle with the totality of human knowledge inside and all of the universe's unknowns on the outside of its thin perimeter. On the segment of the circle pertaining to artificial intelligence, very few researchers are closer to that invisible boundary, energetically hammering to expand it, than Dr. Hasani. His résumé reads like a parent's dream come true, or perhaps something out of a John le Carré novel. He studied electrical engineering as an undergraduate in Iran, earned his master's in electronic engineering in Milan, and then spent time conducting research between Austria and London. When we spoke, he was a postdoctoral associate at MIT's storied Computer Science and AI Lab (CSAIL)—an institution that can trace its lineage back to the '60s cradle of AI study.

Initially, I wanted to get in touch with Hasani to discuss his recent and intriguing contributions to the field of deep learning, but he insisted his "passion was always physics and the relationship to the physical world." Speaking with him underscored for me that AI research can't happen in a vacuum; it's necessarily tied into and informed by other fundamental disciplines like biology, psychology, and physics. When Hasani studied in Milan, he said, "One professor was saying, 'I have this new idea to bring biologically inspired neural networks on-chip. Would you be interested in implementing those kinds of things?' And I was like, 'Whoa, yes. Absolutely.'" But first, what are neural networks?

If they're an alien concept to you, suffice it to say that neural networks are infinitely flexible, somewhat controversial machine learning algorithms whose design is partly inspired by the human brain. The mathematical underpinnings for neural nets date back at least to the '50s, but recent improvements in computing hardware, data collection capabilities, and research budgets in the late nineties and 2000s–2010s propelled neural nets to the fore of the AI and machine learning space. Given enough training data, they can be used for predicting continuous values (such as a car's fuel efficiency), classifying things into discrete categories (like fraudulent or not-fraudulent credit card transactions), clustering similar datapoints into groups (for example, movies similar to ones you've already enjoyed), and more.

Neural networks are intrinsically problematic for some applications because while they can squeeze out better performance than other types of machine learning algorithms, they do so at the expense of explainability. They're frequently called "black-box" models—as in, totally opaque. By their nature, it is challenging to say *why* a neural-net-based model made a particular prediction. That's not the case with simpler machine learning methods, like basic linear regression, where you can plainly see which factors influence the final outcomes. Neural nets do not follow explicitly coded rules. They are fed arrays of example data and asked to make sometimes hundreds, thousands, or more connections between input and output variables "under the hood." It is notoriously challenging to examine and evaluate the significance of these connections and bring them back down to the human level for real-world inference.

Explainability is important. In any critical application, we need to be able to say *why* an automated system acted the way it did. If an algorithm determines that you have a terrible credit score, it needs to be able to tell you what factors tanked that score. You need to be able to determine how to go about fixing your credit score, and the credit bureau needs to be able to justify the score they assigned you. If an algorithm is screening résumés for a busy job recruiter, that recruiter needs to be sure their predictive model has not excluded a candidate simply based on their surname, which could be a proxy for ethnicity. Thus, today's AI research community is in hot pursuit of machine learning models that can perform just as well as the best neural networks— while retaining explainability.

In my estimation, Dr. Hasani is one of the central figures in this search, and nematodes have been important to him.

Certain organisms are particularly well-suited to serve as models through which to study biological processes. The zebrafish has a translucent body, a fully sequenced genome, and easily observable developmental behaviors, making it one of a handful of good examples. The fruit fly researchers and the nematode folks like to go toe to toe; each group likes to lightheartedly claim that theirs is, hands down, the "best" model organism (although, of course, the experimental context matters). Regardless of which species is "best," these animal models play a crucial part in understanding the underlying principles of biology, which is the seat of intelligence—the medium upon which thought first naturally occurred.

Using what he gleaned from the biological research community about the C. elegans (nematode) worm brain, Dr. Hasani and his colleagues developed and implemented what he calls "liquid neural networks." These more closely mimic the adaptability of animal intelligence in computerized systems than previous neural network architectures. Here's how Hasani says he approached this cross-disciplinary osmosis:

> When I realized we have the entire brain of the [C. elegans] mapped, I thought: *Oh my god, the degree of controllability that this system can generate is fascinating!* Then I started talking to Manuel Zimmer, one of the greatest C. elegans neuroscientists in the world. He gave me a lot more insight on how these things work, but then my idea was to get inspiration from there and *run away* because...you get another degree of respect for biologists when you start interacting with them. The work they do requires significant amounts of patience.

Dr. Hasani's research papers laying out new ideas like liquid neural nets have been featured in such publications as

Nature Machine Intelligence, the *Conference on Neural Information Processing Systems* (NeurIPS), the *International Conference on Machine Learning* (ICML), the *International Conference on Robotics and Automation* (ICRA), and more. These are essentially the *Rolling Stone*, *Time Magazine*, and *National Geographic* of the machine learning space. He said, "Brain-inspired networks can be used and can be stacked with any type of deep learning agent. They can be very performant with really, really small numbers of elements in order to perform computations." That's a huge leap forward for explainable AI.

I asked him to define computer vision in as few words as possible. Rising to the challenge, he said, "Computer vision is making computers able to *see* the world and *play* with the world" via that sense of sight. Faced with this question, most respondents were eager to expand their definitions beyond just "seeing" or even comprehending the world to something more two-way. Hasani said, "You enable a computer to see. Based on what it sees, it can decide to *interact* with it or not do anything about it." Sure, watching is often how we learn, but the real reason the current renaissance in computer vision is so exciting is because so many of our *actions* and *reactions* are driven by visual sensory input. That's what stands to be automated.

Hasani doesn't work alone. He has a trusted collaborator and counterpart in programming whiz Mathias Lechner. Hasani said he "was his supervisor for [Lechner's] master's studies in Vienna. We have such an amazing synergy, in terms of getting things done." Hasani distinctly remembers the day he met Lechner:

> We wanted to do parking with the worm's brain. That was the advertisement for a master's thesis, and he

got interested. He came to my office. He's not a very talkative person; he's very shy. So he came and sat in my office. I wanted to interview him because his profile was good. I asked him, "What do you know, in terms of machine learning, research, programming languages" and everything. Then he said one sentence. That's it. He said, "I know C-Sharp." That's all he said.

Not every machine learning engineer would be so bold as to take on this daunting task. It takes a certain sort of tenacious and adventurous spirit to try to automate parallel parking, even with a small remote-controlled car, using a model no more complex than a nematode's humble brain. C-Sharp isn't the easiest programming language to learn and master, either. It offers few of the conveniences that make programming languages like Python so popular. Lechner's laconic response was sort of like when Neo from *The Matrix* said, "I know kung fu" (Wachowski 1999). Hasani's job post attracted exactly the sort of person he was hoping for:

> I realized that the guy is so humble. Every week he was developing stuff for us, any idea we had. He's such a fast programmer. He's so aware of what he is doing. It's just fascinating looking at how he does things. It's very hard to get words out of his mouth. It's usually because he's a very lazy person, and because of his laziness, he gets work done very, very well. He's very smart. He's amazing.

To be called lazy, as a programmer, is high praise. Lazy programmers automate everything they can with code so they don't have to do it twice—thereby becoming great programmers. Hasani said, "Mathias is, I think, by far, the best programmer I've seen in my entire life, even compared to people we have here [at MIT]. That's a high bar." Lechner and Hasani make a dynamic power-duo of theory and execution that's greater than the sum of its parts. Together, they used robotics as a test bed for new concepts, pioneering the budding field of *imitation learning*, which Hasani described as "basically teaching an algorithm how to behave from expert demonstrations," the same way babies learn to walk by watching others walk. He said:

> If you have a human driver, you collect the data from this human driver's behavior. It could be the control actions they take. And you mount some sensors on the car, so you can collect data that are input-outputs. Then you could train a neural network (or any type of algorithm) from data from these demonstrations to mimic the behavior of that agent. This is called imitation learning.

Neural-net-piloted robots don't yet grasp *why* they're optimizing for these utterly specific goals, such as parallel parking accurately. However, Hasani and his crack team of collaborators (such as Lechner) are designing algorithms that capture more of the underlying nature of the tasks at hand. Rather than trying to oversimplify and train in a digital vacuum, these machine learning agents are trained in a three-dimensional environment, where real-world effects come to bear. Dust on the uneven floor, air turbulence from the ceiling fan, imperfect mechanical components, and more such chaos better simulate what a real vehicle might experience on the open road.

The smallness and lightness of these nematode-inspired models is making notoriously opaque neural networks significantly more interpretable. It's easier to map out a nematode's brain than a mouse's, and it's much easier to deconstruct a neural net with just dozens of elements than one with thousands.

However, wherever there is innovation, skeptics inevitably rear their heads. Hasani said his team "had this paper published in *Nature Machine Intelligence*. One reviewer said, 'This is cool research, but I cannot believe that any part of this technology would make its way into real-life products.' And he mentioned that with such confidence, elaborating on it a lot. Now, just one year later, our products are already...getting used in safety-critical applications." Gatekeepers don't always draw their swords for the right reasons! This is a reminder that no matter how valuable and novel whatever you're working on may be, someone will always be there to tell you otherwise. Keep going.

I asked Hasani what he thought about job displacement as a result of increasingly sophisticated AI, particularly for computer vision tasks. If we're headed for a world where algorithms hands-down outperform humans at driving cars, what will former taxi drivers do for a living? Hasani said, "One of the big challenges now is continuing learning....in the education sector, we must have fundamental changes because we have the tools and abilities to do that, for normal people who are already engaged in jobs." Few folks working in machine learning talk about this enough. The tectonic plates of technology are shifting under our feet so quickly now that adults can't be expected to go decades (in any field) without some formalized continuing education programs in place.

The best and brightest can't keep building the future without building a bridge for everyone else to come. That bridge probably looks like a massive overhaul of our education system—from something linear, at just the beginning of our lives, to something more cyclical, for folks of all ages.

Hasani made time to speak with me, despite the fact that he was busy preparing to give a key presentation at the NeurIPS conference two days later, because he sees enormous value in sharing what happens in the ivory tower with as many folks as possible. He said, "Everyday people and lawmakers have to be aware of the process. We have to start with those people." That's the first step in order for us to design tools that take everybody's voices and needs into consideration.

Radically powerful new technologies are useless if they foster too much suspicion and fear to be widely embraced by society. If all people can see are a technology's potential pitfalls, everybody misses out on its material benefits. The more complex the AI system, the harder it is to explain—and the less likely it is to be adequately regulated. We have plenty of work to do in making highly performant computer vision systems simpler and spreading the word about their potential to save us time while doing a great job with critical tasks. That's what Dr. Hasani and his nematode brains are all about.

08

SCREWDRIVERS VERSUS GUNS

John Nack said sometimes he's "up all night with stress because of all the ethical considerations" around computer vision's applications in expressive tech. That's good for the rest of us. We'd be in trouble if the folks partially responsible for making computer vision applications widely available had no regard for the technology's inherent moral dilemmas, of which there are a few.

I'm a longtime student of digital filmmaking, but my rudimentary introduction to computer-aided artistry was playing with a program called "kid pix" in computer lab at elementary school. Nack has a few years on me. He told me:

> As a kid, when I saw Mac Paint for the first time at my friend's birthday party, it was just like a road to Damascus moment. It was obviously not computer vision like we'd recognize today, but like, fundamentally, painting on the screen, and procedurally filling regions, making selections...it's all the same grammar. And I remember when I saw Photoshop for the first time.

Nack said he's "been a product manager since Bill Clinton was president, which freaks me out. Now I'm trying to advise college kids who probably weren't alive then." He "spent about ten years on Photoshop and getting it to mobile. My last year and a half, two years was back in video, trying to help people do storytelling. I ended up at Google because they were proposing to do this kind of work but at a truly massive scale, like applying computer vision for a billion people." Any computer engineering challenge ratchets up in difficulty by several orders of magnitude when you move from tinkering and experimentation into "production," or attempting to make a service widely available and reliable for the masses.

In one's career, Nack said, "You get to pick kind of a mission bio. I always said mine was 'teaching Google Photoshop.' I want this computer to *see like I can*—not to replace me or other humans but to give a massively larger number of people access to the kind of creativity, or creative output, that I would like and get a lot of dumb crap out of my way so I can focus on the more distinctive interesting stuff. It was an interesting journey."

Today, as a product manager at Adobe's AI division (called "Sensei"), Nack's work is to "continue to break new ground and make things that are exciting and relevant" in a world where mobile photo manipulation app Facetune, with its nearly thirty million monthly active users, has been recently valued at $1.8 billion (Perez 2021).

Nack and his cohort are working hard to bring the latest and greatest computer vision tools to the masses, despite the fact that it's an ethical minefield, because they know how revolutionary it can be when expressive technology is democratized. When the latest creative software tools make their way into the hands of students and cultures around the world, it enables art to emerge from new places and from people who previously had fewer ways to express themselves.

For Nack, "part of the exciting mission is to go and understand like what you can do with GANs. You know, what can you do by combining machine learning and traditional computer vision, and devising a pipeline where folks can mix and match things to hopefully be creative in ways that they can't as readily with apps that are very one-stop." In his previous role at Google, Nack and his colleagues were "commoditizing and automating a lot of magic that used to take a highly skilled operator to do. I think that's the march of progress. It's on Adobe and other toolmakers to keep running ahead of that, which is hard but hopefully fun."

So how do folks like Nack and organizations like Adobe navigate the moral quandaries at the tip of the technological spear? How do you act as an arbiter, holding the keys to new capabilities that could have sweeping effects on society? Why should they care, besides the fact that John Nack loses sleep at night? He told me, "There's tech Adobe has never shipped because that's part of the calculus."

Let's step outside of computer science for a moment and talk about makeup. Is makeup morally problematic? Not inherently. Makeup is mostly just a bunch of emulsifiers, preservatives, and coloring agents. However, as with most ethical questions, context matters, and we must consider nuances. You could ask where the coloring agents come from. An animal? A mine?

And how did that makeup make its way to you—through fair trade, or exploitation? What about the pharmaceutical drugs that have fueled an opioid epidemic? Are they inherently evil? Oxycodone is just a well-engineered narcotic analgesic medicine until its overuse by an unwell society with poor safeguards makes it a problem.

This is not to say that our society is fighting a makeup epidemic. As exploitative or unsustainable as the cosmetic industry may or may not be, "digital makeup," which requires no single-use plastic packaging, has already become a widespread part of online culture. Like facial recognition, it bears the potential to help us out in a number of benign use cases. However, as with any new technology, it has the potential to hurt us if we're not mindful about how it's designed, implemented, and distributed.

Facetune is a mobile photo-editing app with fairly state-of-the-art, computer-vision-powered (but dead-easy) features like tooth whitening, skin smoothing, and pimple removal. Between 2010 and 2018, Facetune spent many days as the number one paid iPhone app, more than almost any other app—roughly 50 percent more days than WhatsApp, and nearly as many as the popular game Minecraft (Nelson 2018).

Nack recognizes that "many millions of people use Facetune. You can debate the ethical or cultural dimensions, but it's not like people don't wear makeup. Right? And it's the same essential thing, in a lot of ways. It's like, well, you comb your hair, you brush your teeth, you put on makeup, and in the same way, you zap zits with digital makeup." Ethical questions arise when it comes to controversial features like skin whitening, and the general body dysphoria that results when young people are invited to create and share augmented, "improved" images of themselves.

Adobe and its flagship product, Photoshop, have long been central to any discussion about representations of beauty augmented by digital manipulation. Those in advertising have had to reckon with the question of "how much airbrushing is too much" for decades. The new question, as computer-vision-enabled tools seep into the mainstream, is this: How easy is too easy, when it comes to touching up your selfies? Whose responsibility is it to draw the line? How might this constitute a problem?

Previously, not everyone could afford to commission a photoshop expert to do things such as elongate their legs and whiten their teeth, and even then, the retoucher had to sign off on the final product—with their own human criteria for what's "normal" and what's pushing the boundaries of realism. Now, since tools like Facetune can be downloaded, installed, and used in minutes or seconds, that friction has been drastically eased. People can tweak their digital body images liberally, with no gatekeeper or ad agency representative to question their artistic license. The paid version of Facetune is sufficient to satisfy the needs of many Instagramers, TikTokers, and users of other popular photo-and-video-sharing apps.

The danger of super-accessible, automatic digital beautification is neither imaginary nor trivial. One article titled "Selfies, Surgeries and Self-Loathing: Inside the Facetune Epidemic" details how such powerful and easy-to-use photo retouching apps as Facetune are causing new levels of widespread body dysmorphic disorder in young users (Cook 2021). Users come to love (or at least accept) the way they look, but only through the distorted filter of the app; the delta between that augmented digital image and the reality of their actual physical bodies is, tragically, driving unprecedented growth in the cosmetic surgery industry.

In 2021, a trove of internal documents known as the Facebook Papers were leaked, exposing Facebook's awareness of similar issues on Instagram, another filter-centric photo sharing app, which they own. *The Wall Street Journal* broke a story about a 2020 slide presentation posted to Facebook's internal message board, which revealed that "32 percent of teen girls said that when they felt bad about their bodies, Instagram made them feel worse" (Wells et al. 2021). Additionally, one internal Facebook slide deck from 2019 pointed out that "we make body image issues worse for one in three teen girls" (Wells et al. 2021).

The ubiquity of selfie-enhancement tools like Facetune has even spawned a new vocabulary. The term "catfish" has come to mean something new. To catfish, in this context, means to edit one's digital appearance to the extent that it's a clean break from reality. Drag a slider to slim your waistline a bit too much, nudge your eyebrows a little too far up your forehead, and you're catfishing. You don't want to be caught in the act; it's dishonest, and it points to your self-consciousness.

Blackface is racist and offensive, so why would a digital implementation of blackface be any less reprehensible? A household-name celebrity of our day, Khloé Kardashian, has come under fire repeatedly for "blackfishing," a subgenre of catfishing where one darkens one's skin to the extent that it becomes cultural appropriation (Spina 2021). She may have used a professional retoucher (or a team) to accomplish this morally dubious effect, but anybody with an iPhone can download the Skin Tone Booth app on the Apple app store today, which, per the app store description, "easily allows you to adjust your skin tone and get that perfect skin color...lighten and darken options available" (Revosoft Technologies 2019).

It is incumbent on software architects to design applications in such a way that minimizes user harm and harmful repurposing. You could argue that "guns don't kill people. People kill people"—but nobody has to feverishly insist that "screwdrivers don't kill people" because a screwdriver's design doesn't suggest utilization as a murder weapon. Simply put, engineers and organizations should design computer vision applications more like screwdrivers and less like guns. Apps like Facetune walk a thin line near the edge of what's acceptable.

Nack said:

> You don't want to do things like FaceApp did four years ago, where they had an ethnicity filter, like here's Trump, and here's him Indian, Black, and Asian, and people immediately freaked out. So...is it creative? Or could it be used creatively? Where you draw the lines isn't always as clear as I might hope.

In some scenarios using an app like Skin Tone Booth isn't necessarily problematic. Cameras are flawed, and lighting conditions are variable. A photo may sincerely require adjustment to more closely match reality. Similar to Nack's point about people wearing makeup daily, some folks frequent tanning salons and wear spray tans, harming nobody. The trouble arises when software companies like the one that publishes Skin Tone Booth enable users to slide that skin color slider as far as they want to, and then they do, in front of a massive social media audience. What can software designers do to preclude use cases that tip over the moral edge?

THE GUNS

As computer vision creates new possibilities in the automatic manipulation of images, we face a number of ethical quandaries beyond the rising tide of body dysmorphic disorder. Nack is acutely aware of them, and he's doing his best to help steer Adobe down the straight and narrow path. He says he's "trying to figure out what AI-first creativity can mean, which...could be hopefully many good things and could be some bad ones if we're not careful."

Nack said, "Photoshop has always let you do things like change a scene or swap a face. Well what's curious, I think, are two things. One is degree of opinionation in the software, in terms of: How much does it become like a human, like an artist? And then based on that, how much responsibility does it have, or do you as the toolmaker have?" The debate around generative models is one very extreme articulation of this quandary.

This hearkens back to the discussion on autonomous vehicles. When systems, even creative systems, are automated, some of the moral imperative gets shifted from the end users back to the tool's designers. When a human picks up a regular old pencil and draws something offensive, it's the artist's fault. That pencil's manufacturer had nothing to do with the artist's bigotry. On the other hand, imagine the pencil is a magic smart-pencil, equipped to draw elaborate forms automatically. The artist simply tells the pencil what to draw and passes off its work as his own. To what extent are the magic pencil's designers responsible when this results in celebrity porn? How should accountability be most fairly distributed?

It takes more or less imagination and effort to re-purpose certain tools for harm. When it comes to harmful use cases of computer vision, certain tools are more like guns than others, such as the erosion of privacy that comes with facial recognition and the fraudulent potential of deepfakes. These, in my estimation, are the biggest "gun" incarnations of computer vision. But what is a deepfake, for the uninitiated?

Deepfakes are synthetic media in which a person in an existing image or video is replaced with someone else's likeness (Witness Media Lab 2022). Last year, "a rendering of the Ukrainian president appearing to tell his soldiers to lay down their arms and surrender the fight against Russia" made headlines in one of the first marquee demonstrations of generative computer vision's potential for abuse (Allyn 2022). With an attentive eye, it's still fairly easy to recognize today's deepfakes—due to certain giveaways, like the tendency not to blink very much, or flyaway hairs unattached to the head—but we're approaching an inflection point where the average unsuspecting media consumer will not be able to ferret them out without expert (human or algorithmic) help.

Deepfakes mark a new low in cyber-bullying as well. "Indeed, the very term 'deepfake' is derived from the username of an anonymous Reddit contributor who began posting manipulated videos of female celebrities in pornographic scenes in 2017" (O'Sullivan 2023). Now you don't even have to be particularly famous to potentially discover, one day, that someone has generated a trove of compromising imagery—of you, performing depraved acts, things you would never do, for the world to see.

Pornographic websites have had to bolster their automatic and manual content moderation capabilities to weed out celebrity deepfakes before they become larger legal problems. An uptick in such deepfake bullying may become one of the greatest scourges that comes with the rising tide of computer vision's accelerated advancement.

For further reading on related societal risks, consider picking up a copy of Nina Schick's *Deepfakes: The Coming Infocalypse*. Call me naively optimistic, but my projection is that because the human spirit is fundamentally good, we will find novel ways to collectively triumph over the looming evils of generative art abuse. The scum will never be completely eradicated, because the tech is already as freely available as oxygen, and bad actors will always crop up. That said, we're building technological and regulatory hurdles to keep malicious material relegated further out onto the seediest corners of the web. Those hurdles will be overcome by bad actors and then bolstered in a continuous cat-and-mouse game.

Nack said his "wife works in the video group, and they have speech synthesis tech, which certainly could be used to deal with gaps and 'uhms' and 'ahhs' and make it smoother." As a former video editor, that sounds great! I've wished many times that I could make the end of someone's sentence sound cleaner and less awkward in interviews. Nack is hopeful that "maybe they'll find a way to just narrowly tailor it. But as a general bit of tech, it can make you say things you didn't say." It would make Adobe look terrible, as a business, to enable people to synthesize whole new Obama speeches (perhaps with offensive pro-Nazi language) with their software. That's not how they want their users to act, so they've kept that capability out of their software, at least for now.

"It doesn't mean if Adobe doesn't play, no one will. It's out there. People can do it...but we will certainly not deploy all the things you could do...somewhere we'll draw a line, and we'll say these things are in, and these ones are out, and we're trying to have a good thorough vetting." This seems to be Adobe's current approach. Introduce new, intelligent tools but slowly, in parts. It's one thing to enable users to type out some text description and generate whatever resulting images they like, with whoever's faces attached. It's safer to give users the ability to do smaller things first, like subtly augmenting a model's pose or de-blurring an image. Companies like Adobe have a brand image to protect, and damaging that image by releasing "guns" could lead to significant loss of revenue, or worse—increased regulatory woes.

A software purveyor can't control what a user does with the tool they create, especially in the open-source world; this is probably the only downside to open-source software. What they *can* do is build the tool to suggest a very specific and constructive use case. If you build your program more like a screwdriver than a gun, people will probably be more inclined to fix things and build new things with it—and less likely to weaponize it, inadvertently or intentionally. That said, based on our varying lived experiences, what looks like a screwdriver to you may feel more like a gun to me. That's where effective regulatory policy has to fill the gaps.

09

LUDDITES AND TROGLODYTES

Maybe you've heard the term "troglodyte"—but do you know its roots? "*Trōglē* may sound like a scary cave-dwelling ogre, but it's actually just a perfectly unintimidating Greek root that means 'hole' or 'cave'" (Merriam-Webster.com). When it comes to the tide of technological advancement, sometimes a big wave appears on the horizon. Not everyone is equipped and excited to grab their surfboards and ride it. Troglodytes tend to stay in their holes, ignoring the wave as it crashes over them. Modern Luddites wage war on the wave. Neither camp does much to slow the tide.

Why do some folks quixotically resist the steady forward march of technological progress? Humans are naturally afraid of the unfamiliar, of change. The future inevitably brings about change. Computer vision is coming for some of our jobs, but maybe that's okay in the long run.

The nineteenth century's industrial revolution completely redefined the landscape of human work, at a more astounding rate than perhaps ever before in human history. However, it may surprise some to learn that the original Luddites were actually not more concerned than the average worker about losing their jobs to automation:

The Luddites themselves "were totally fine with machines," says Kevin Binfield, editor of the 2004 collection *Writings of the Luddites.* They confined their attacks to manufacturers who used machines in what they called "a fraudulent and deceitful manner" to get around standard labor practices. "They just wanted machines that made high-quality goods," says Binfield, "and they wanted these machines to be run by workers who had gone through an apprenticeship and got paid decent wages" (Conniff 2011).

The original Luddites were actually pretty relatable. As misunderstood as they are today, their protests took the form of breaking knitting machines and burning the occasional factory, which is the part of their legacy that stuck. Their efforts were eventually squashed with legal and military might, but the term Luddite still serves to describe anybody generally skeptical of or resistant to new technologies.

Just as textile production machines displaced weavers in the nineteenth century, increasingly capable computer vision technologies will continue to relieve humans from performing repetitive tasks that are too dangerous, boring, or time-consuming to pay a human to do. Modern Luddites and Troglodytes should feel invited to ride that wave with the rest of us, even if their initial reactions to change come from a place of justifiable fear or distrust. Let's work together to remove the root causes of that fear, building buffers for folks who will be adversely impacted by the rising tide.

Technological change may carry the promise to alleviate certain societal woes, but it may also result in painful transitionary periods for many. Understandably, people are especially afraid of changes that will make their jobs obsolete. It may be too late in life for, say, a factory worker, made redundant by a computer-vision-enabled robot, to pick up an entirely new and more technical skillset. Spending time and money on continued education may not be within their means. For many, an unexpected lapse in employment could spell economic ruin. AI and computer vision will continue to steal jobs from human laborers, and those left unemployed will not be evenly distributed by age and ethnicity.

In 350 BCE, Aristotle surmised in his famous treatise *Politics* that "if…the shuttle would weave and the plectrum touch the lyre without a hand to guide them, chief workmen would not want servants, nor masters slaves" (Aristotle 2017). In this instance Aristotle was wrong. Today, the shuttle indeed weaves without a hand to guide it, but demand for menial labor hasn't gone anywhere. The lyre has given way to Spotify, but we still live in a society with armies of food delivery workers, ride-share drivers, and freelancers who will build your Ikea furniture. As we automate more jobs, we free up chunks of humanity's aggregate time and energy. That simultaneously increases our collective quality of life (forever) and swells the available supply of human labor, devaluing it (temporarily).

History repeats itself. Lyft estimated that they conservatively had one million active drivers using their platform in 2020 (Lemar 2021). Uber had about three million in 2021 (Lemar 2022). That's at least four million ride-share drivers operating without the guidance of human dispatchers and counting. Uber, Lyft, and other ride-sharing apps haven't automated the job of driving the actual car yet, but what are taxi dispatchers doing for work now? Dispatching is the job that Uber and Lyft *really* automated away. Drivers just suffer the downstream consequences.

During a recent Lyft ride, a driver told me that he'd left his job with a limousine company because the dispatchers were shamelessly corrupt. He said that as a limo driver, you could only get enough rides to make a profit if you paid off the dispatchers in a form of extortion. Since the advent of automated dispatching, the supply of human dispatcher labor has become so great that the dollar value of their services has plummeted. Thus the turn to corruption, at least in this one case. AI-enabled apps suffice for most driver-passenger coordination, so who's still paying humans to do it? A smattering of elite limousine services, who want to provide a personal touch? Certainly not enough of them to sustain a whole profession.

Taxi dispatchers haven't gone quite as extinct as elevator operators yet, but I'd still call them victims of "technological unemployment," the loss of jobs caused by technological change. I feel for the Luddites. They had an honest way to make a decent living, which evaporated in a flash when their calculating provincial overlords replaced them with machines at the drop of a hat. Much more of this has happened since, and much more will come soon. Let's prepare.

Even the word "computer" shifted from a human job title—mostly women running manual calculations—to a name for a machine. I hope during my lifetime, "driver" becomes, primarily, a word you use in reference to the computer system piloting your car. Human ride-share and freight drivers will need new jobs because as valuable as their work is today, few passengers will want to pay more for a more dangerous ride. It will be bad news for at least four million souls when robo-taxies become more reliable than human-operated ones but good for humanity in the long term. Immeasurable work-hours will be redirected—for the living and as-yet unborn alike. People will get around more safely, inexpensively, and quickly.

Regarding the rise of technological unemployment, Google cofounder Larry Page said that "even if there's going to be a disruption on people's jobs, in the short term that's likely to be made up by the decreasing cost of things we need, which I think is really important and not being talked about" (Waters 2014). His perspective may be marginally skewed, as one of the richest people I can think of. Nevertheless, in a future where getting a ride is markedly cheaper, we'll all have a little more mobility, and money saved for the rest of our expenses. The same is true of produce, T-shirts, or cars. The more automation in the production pipeline, the cheaper the product, and the more capital is freed up to live the rest of our lives.

Banning emerging technologies to spare the Luddites only works for so long. Eventually the undeniable broader advantages of automation outweigh the plea of the technologically unemployed, and societies leave Luddites stranded. Gandhi proposed a delay in the uptake of labor-saving machines until unemployment was alleviated, an idea that was implemented in the twentieth century within China under Mao's administration (Gandhi 2023). Compromises like these could see a resurgence as broader swaths of working-class people are swept into job limbo. There must be some way to tap the brakes on a disruptive technology while we build the social safety net for those whose lives will be disrupted.

Only a tiny minority of political economists believe that stopping or slowing the tide of technology is a viable way to prevent net job losses due to technological unemployment (Blaug 1997). More viable solutions include commissioning public works or (my favorite) reforming education. If the government commissions ambitious projects, as FDR's Works Progress Administration did in the wake of the great depression, more folks become employed in the enhancement of their own society.

If our education system is retooled on the assumption that folks will need re-skilling at least every ten years, we'll be more resilient to technological unemployment. The shelf lives of hard job skills are shrinking. Lower-cost, shorter-running tech "bootcamps" have started to capitalize on this pain point, but we also need to develop analogous training programs for careers outside of computer programming.

Why else might the average American harbor distrust of AI and computer vision, aside from the fact that they may be threatening their livelihood?

News media tends to gravitate toward things that have already gone wrong. Similarly, it's challenging to make a great movie, or at least one that sells, where everything is peachy and utopic. Conflict is the stuff that great stories are made of. Science fiction films like *Blade Runner, I, Robot*, and *Minority Report* don't offer much comfort in their imaginings of futures where AI is ubiquitous. *Ex Machina* also leans toward horror and pessimism, and the performances are stunning. While cautionary tales are important to help us avoid pitfalls, and they're entertaining, they're not necessarily striving for the purest, most level-headed realism. That tendency in our pop culture subconscious can make it more challenging to have optimistic conversations about technology.

By contrast, Spike Jonze's 2013 movie, *Her*, serves as a sober counterpoint. The film validates our day-to-day problems, subtly reflecting on the human condition and projecting it into a future where mature general AI has proliferated. Notably, cars are nowhere to be seen throughout the movie—the natural next step for metropolitan centers, after we make most cars electric and pilot themselves. *Her* refuses to default to a played-out, worst-case-scenario AI dystopia, suggesting that super-advanced AI may be more likely to break hearts than bones once we get there.

Pop culture has not tended to cast AI in a positive light. That wouldn't make for good TV.

There's also the looming presence of tech mega-corporations like Google, whose motto was once "don't be evil" but has since changed.

We live in politically divisive times, but both sides of the aisle have found reasons to distrust the enormous tech entities of our day. Almost 60 percent of Americans surveyed said they support breaking up Big Tech monopolies: "Those on the right have lambasted Big Tech for perceived censorship, while those on the left have accused companies like Facebook and Google of stoking online extremism" (Molla 2021). The same contentious mega-corps are also some of the greatest epicenters of AI and computer vision advancement, arguably more so than the Ivy League institutions that initially pioneered the field. My suspicion is that folks have grown leery of AI partly just because it emerges from these entities, whose ontological purposes are to maximize shareholder value.

While Big Tech companies rake in preposterous revenue numbers and skirt taxation, they also find ways to make positive contributions to the broader AI research community. Google released the popular open-source TensorFlow machine learning software library in 2015, empowering students and organizations to train their own deep learning models with dramatically less friction. It's what I used to train my first "Santa Claus or not" image classification model.

Facebook (now Meta) collaborated with the open-source community and Microsoft to respond with their own free deep learning framework, PyTorch, which has since eclipsed TensorFlow as one of the most popular tools for AI researchers and engineers at all skill levels. Meta and Microsoft have since transferred PyTorch's governance to the Linux Foundation, which is like the Switzerland of computer science, serving as a neutral arbiter focused on cooperation and open access. Millions of tinkerers, entrepreneurs, and scientists wouldn't be using deep learning to our society's benefit if not for these generalized tools, which are as free now as the air we breathe.

Google uses AI for "detecting locust outbreaks which threaten food security and livelihoods for millions of people," and "machine-learning-based forecasting to provide over 360 million people with alerts about upcoming floods" (Manyika 2022). They release state-of-the-art research papers on computer vision and natural language processing methods as well as enormous pretrained models, inviting the rest of us to experiment and expand our collective capabilities. This is not an argument that Big Tech companies are good on aggregate—just that they do some good things with AI, and AI isn't what makes them evil, if they are.

We should absolutely break up behemoth businesses when they exhibit monopolistic tendencies, but powerful AI tools aren't what turn companies into market bullies. I have no problem with Amazon's terrific product recommendation engine. I like that I can find what I need quickly. I just hate that they go out of their way to give their own branded products priority in the same marketplace as the mom-and-pop sellers on the same site, extorting them for advertising revenue. By the way, Amazon holds a patent for floating fulfillment warehouses in the sky. I'm not sure how I would feel about my consumer experience looking more like the 1915 German zeppelin bombing of London. Call me a troglodyte in some aspects.

The scariest thing about Tesla is not that their cars, which use computer vision to build models of their surroundings, glitch out and crash sometimes. What frightens me more is that their CEO was once excited to open a new Tesla showroom in Xinjiang, an area of China where "crimes against humanity include imprisonment, torture, rape, forced sterilization, and persecution" (Dunleavy 2021). The Uyghur genocide may be the largest-scale detention of ethnic and religious minorities since World War II, but our titans of industry still smell market opportunities (Kirby 2020).

If a car company's underbaked self-driving feature kills people, it's not because there's some inherent evil in AI. Deep learning is mostly just a bunch of carefully sequenced matrix multiplications. The problem is more that corporations tend to value sales over the safety of their customers, at least until they're pressured—either economically (via bad press affecting sales), or directly (through regulation)—to remedy that.

Corporations blitz out disruptive new technologies without considering—or perhaps even caring—about the potential second-order social side effects, causing collateral damage. As technologies find widespread adoption, they tend to liberate the masses from tedium and suffering. Modern luddites and troglodytes may be better off directing their ire at those who would use powerful new technologies to undercut the vulnerable, rather than at the technology itself. On the other hand, we could all be a bit more like the original Luddites of yore, demanding fair pay and quality over quantity.

10

BIG BROTHER

You can unlock your phone just by showing it your face. What if you could pay your bus or train fare with just your face?

In Russia, you can. In October of 2021, Moscow's "cashless, cardless, and phoneless system, named Face Pay, launched at more than 240 [metro] stations across the Russian capital" (Sauer 2021). Futuristic, right? The marginal convenience of not having to fumble in your pockets for something to swipe or tap for admission comes, of course, at a steep cost. The tired Silicon Valley refrain is that if the service is free, you, the user, are the product. However, there are worse fates than being packaged and sold as a data product.

In 2021, a Russian photo blogger named "Georgy Malets didn't make it to an anti-Kremlin rally... He was detained on his way there by police using facial recognition technology in the Moscow metro" (Stolyarov 2021). In his case, Malets didn't even have to register for Face Pay and upload images of himself before they were used against him. The police identified him with a photograph from one of his social network profiles. The facial recognition payment infrastructure's mere existence enabled the state to detain and silence this journalist. His was not an isolated incident.

Violating a long-standing taboo, "in 2016, a Russian company called NTechLab developed a facial-recognition algorithm… which matched photos of strangers to profiles on VK—essentially Russia's Facebook" (Hill 2021). It wasn't long before their app's users "were using the app to identify sex workers, porn stars and protesters," so now NTechLab only licenses their algorithm to governments and corporations. In Moscow, when this "was repurposed to enforce lockdown during the Covid-19 pandemic… In March, a man who was supposed to be quarantining went outside his apartment to take out the trash; thirty minutes later, the police were at his door." I don't want to be part of a society where police have that kind of overarching power with ever-vigilant eyes on everybody's comings and goings from home, work, and everywhere.

It has some helpful use cases, but facial recognition has become, easily, computer vision's most problematic application.

It can be challenging to fathom the loss of privacy that comes with publishing your "faceprint," or the biometric data that ties your face to your identity. In direct-to-consumer genetic testing, you spit in a tube and send it to a company like 23andMe. They may decide to resell your genetic information down the line, but at least they're the only ones holding the goods, for now. If you upload your profile picture to a public-facing social media profile, however, you have in a sense given everyone access to a piece of your biometric data. This wouldn't be much of a problem if facial recognition systems weren't becoming so eye-poppingly performant.

To this day, "no federal law limits the use of genetic information by life insurance companies" (Huddleston 2023).

Companies like 23andMe should be paying their "customers" (read: products) for the genetic data they bundle en masse and resell to insurance providers and other interested parties. The contours of your face carry similar value. They're a commodity, tightly coupled to the rest of your identity, and they're pretty difficult to retract once you've given them away. Unlike your home address and phone number, you can't change your DNA at will. At least there's plastic surgery for your face.

That said, aren't there at least *some* positive use cases for facial recognition? Would good people pursue advances in this field if there was zero potential for a utilitarian upside?

For one, facial recognition can create convenience. It is convenient to be able to unlock your phone by simply pointing it at your face rather than relying on a smudge-prone fingerprint scanner, or heavens forbid, needing to enter your four-digit passcode. A facial-recognition-based secure entry system at a sensitive place of work, like a mental hospital, is preferable to nothing. There is no keycard to melt in the dryer if your face is the key.

Every facial recognition pro has its corresponding con. What if your face is the key to something really important?

> The FBI searched the house of twenty-eight-year-old Grant Michalski...who would later that month be charged with receiving and possessing child pornography. With a search warrant in hand, a federal investigator told Michalski to put his face in front of the phone, which he duly did. That allowed the agent to pick through the suspect's online chats, photos and

whatever else he deemed worthy of investigation"
(Brewster 2018).

This spurs a whole new discussion around Fifth Amendment
rights. Is this an example of a new form of self-incrimination,
and should there be protections against it? I'm glad they caught
this one child pornographer, but I suspect variations on this
theme will become less black-and-white as we roll into the
mid-twenty-first century. Facial recognition isn't a perfect
security system, which could spell bad things for good people.

While we're still driving the cars ourselves, how would you
like to unlock and start yours with facial recognition? In 2019,
"Apple obtained the rights to a facial recognition system that
would allow your car to recognize you as you approach. Such
a system would let cars unlock their doors when they see a
registered user approach—and maybe even remember how
each person likes to position the driver's seat and mirrors"
(Robitzski 2019). I'd be okay with that, if I owned a car, as long
as my biometric data stayed locally siloed to the car and off
of Apple's servers.

If the proper security and privacy measures are in place, the
convenience can be worth the risk of digitizing my biometric
data. Problems emerge when my faceprint is made public or
collected and stored with millions of others on some centralized server. Despite careful security measures, these sorts
of datasets are highly valuable and thus big targets for data
theft. The medical industry understands the value of siloing
data, perhaps too well. Many have failed in the struggle to
transfer even their own medical records from one provider's
database to another's. There needs to be a little bit more of

that healthy caution when it comes to our faceprints because while they're not quite as revealing as genes, there's plenty to learn from when and where your face appears in the wild.

Speaking of genetics, an app called Face2Gene leverages a machine learning algorithm to analyze faces "to suggest genetic disorders a person might have" (Simonite 2022). Now thousands of geneticists worldwide use the app to assist in diagnosing rare conditions and even compare patients' faces between continents to identify conditions for which data is incredibly scarce or non-existent. This seems like a fairly harmless application of facial recognition, but the key word here is "suggest." No algorithm is perfect, so it's important that clinicians continue to use this as a tool for hints rather than an end-all be-all diagnosis solution. The potential for data breaches is no less considerable here than in any other medical context.

Even if your town institutes a municipal ban on facial recognition technology, like the one enacted by San Francisco in 2019, that only "prohibits city agencies from using facial recognition technology, or information gleaned from external systems that use the technology" (Conger et al. 2019). It does not bar private institutions from implementing facial recognition systems in, say, their retail stores.

For example, in a city where facial recognition is "banned" for the police, the supermarket might still decide to use facial recognition to identify recurrent shoplifters or validate credit card payments with biometrics. Facial recognition may be used by retailers to collect age, gender, and ethnicity data on shoppers, even if they don't end up purchasing anything during their visit. Cities need more comprehensive policies than simple bans.

Casinos are home to at least a couple of interesting facial recognition applications. "Many casinos in the US use facial recognition to detect blacklisted card-counters and cheaters," surprising nobody (Nott 2019). Casinos have total control over their internal environment and will do everything in their power to mitigate losses; the house, famously, always wins. What I didn't know was that "casinos and clubs in Australia must by law provide the option for customers to 'self-exclude' themselves from a venue, as a way of supporting individuals whose gambling has become a problem. During the self-exclusion process, a minimum ban period is agreed and a photo taken." They use facial recognition to keep recovering gambling addicts away from their greatest temptation.

NEC is one of the biggest players in the commercial facial recognition industry. At one casino, NEC's facial recognition system "detected [a] man trying to enter the premises, even though he had previously requested he be turned away... The man tried on two more occasions to gain entry by attempting to disguise his appearance. It didn't work" (Nott 2019). For the sake of those with stubborn gambling habits, ones they're trying to kick, I'm glad facial recognition has gotten good enough to spot them—even when in disguise.

Facial recognition carries the potential to boost public safety somewhat, at the sharp risk of encroaching on privacy. For instance, when a man was apprehended for shooting and killing five in a Maryland newsroom, "he refused to divulge his name. So the authorities identified the man...using a different method: facial recognition" (Metz and Singer 2018).

Members of the public identified Capitol insurrectionists with facial recognition. When a violent criminal remains at large, facial recognition applied to security camera or other footage could offer clues to triangulate them quickly before they cause more harm.

In a crowd context like a stadium or an international port, where there are already security checkpoints and body scanners, it's understood that you essentially waive much of your privacy just by passing through. In the absence of thoughtful oversight policies and enforcement, systems like these are abused, suppressing our established freedoms.

If and when we nail the regulatory policies, however, it will be more helpful than harmful to allow facial recognition systems to watch out for known bad actors, especially in places where they could do massive damage. Airports, for example, could be required to collect and release statistics detailing the demographics of the folks they "randomly" search, or stop and search based on facial recognition matches, to identify and discourage racial profiling. We have to find ways to get the best of both worlds, maximizing the fair utility of computer vision while preventing its abuse by authority figures.

We can locate missing persons faster with facial recognition. There is no need to add their photo to any centralized missing persons image database until they do, in fact, go missing. Then when their face shows up in the backseat of a car at a gas station, the system could alert the authorities to investigate. Again, we just need to prevent crooked cops from abusing these kinds of systems to stalk their crushes, for example.

Facial recognition saves toilet paper. "Chinese authorities in Beijing are now combating a toilet paper stealing epidemic by locking the supplies away behind a dispenser powered by facial recognition software" (Statt 2017). You present your face to a wall-mounted machine to get two feet of TP, which can be repeated by individuals every nine minutes. Custodial staff have gone from replacing fourteen rolls of toilet paper per dispenser per day to just four. This is not totally ideal, since that may not be sufficient toilet paper for some, and one has to remember to proactively visit the dispenser before entering a toilet stall. At least there aren't cameras in the stalls themselves yet.

China's moral depravity in utilizing surveillance technology to oppress ethnic minorities catastrophically outweighs their savings in toilet paper. In the Xinjiang region, the state uses facial recognition for "automatically flagging the faces of Uighurs and other ethnic minorities and tracking their comings and goings. In 2018, Chinese police officers began testing out facial-recognition glasses that would let them more easily ID the people they interact with" (Hill 2021). People feared exactly this sort of dystopian future when Google Glass was first unveiled. A million plus citizens are penned in by a mesh of surveillance technology. Attempted escapees are shot or worse. In a region that produces one fifth of the world's cotton, hundreds of thousands of laborers are forced to pick it. China is degrading and eradicating a whole culture for their ethnicity and religion, and facial recognition is making it all much more efficient. That's about as bad as it gets, as far as computer vision's potential for evil.

Countless American police departments have already commissioned the services of facial recognition companies, like the infamous Clearview AI, to help identify perpetrators of crimes from footage—a seemingly noble end via dubious means.

Clearview AI had scraped billions of images from the internet to create a facial recognition database… Clearview's massive surveillance apparatus claims to hold 3 billion photos, accessible to any law enforcement agency with a subscription, and it's likely you or people you know have been scooped up in the company's dragnet. It's known to have scraped sites like Facebook, LinkedIn, YouTube, and Instagram, and is able to use profile names and associated images to build a trove of identified and scannable facial images (Gershgorn 2021).

If you've uploaded a photo of yourself to one of those platforms, your face is probably in Clearview's database. Monolithic platforms like Facebook have done little more than to send strongly worded letters in the hopes of discouraging Clearview from further such data collection efforts. They are effectively powerless to prevent this.

Kashmir Hill is *the* reporter to follow on today's facial recognition and data privacy beat. She covered the story of Robert Julian-Borchak Williams, which "may be the first known account of an American being wrongfully arrested based on a flawed match from a facial recognition algorithm" (Hill 2020). Imagine the cold, brightly lit interrogation room where Williams sat with two detectives:

"Is this you?" asked the detective. The second piece of paper was a close-up. The photo was blurry, but it was clearly not Mr. Williams.

He picked up the image and held it next to his face. "No, this is not me," Mr. Williams said. "You think all black men look alike?"

The two detectives leaned back in their chairs and looked at one another. One detective, seeming chagrined, said to his partner: "I guess the computer got it wrong" (Hill 2020).

Just because law enforcement agencies are willing to pay for a computer vision tool doesn't mean it works well. Most facial recognition systems are notoriously worse at discerning between people of color, and they're not always fed the highest-quality images possible. Paired with lazy police work, you end up with situations like Mr. Williams'. He was arrested in front of his family at home, forced to spend the night in detention, and deeply humiliated by the occurrence. This, tragically, is not even a worst-case outcome for a "very large" black man in an encounter with American police.

How will we, as a society, decide what margin of error is acceptable in the pursuit of the "bad guys" with facial recognition? Is there an ethical way to build a database of people's faces, if they haven't all given their explicit permission?

As far as investors are concerned, the moral quagmire that is facial recognition smells like a great bet. In the first two months of 2021, investors "funneled hundreds of millions into several facial recognition startups. A breakdown of Crunchbase data...shows a sharp rise in venture funding in facial recognition companies at well over $500 million in 2021 so far [by July], compared to $622 million for all of 2020" (Whittaker 2021). Many investors in this space prefer not to be identified. Gratefully, in June of 2021, "a group of fifty investors with more than $4.5 trillion in assets called on dozens of facial recognition companies, including Amazon, Facebook, Alibaba and Huawei, to build their technologies ethically" (Whittaker 2021). Where they place their bets will be more telling than their platitudes. Maybe some of that mind-bogglingly gargantuan stockpile of assets could go toward building less Anglocentric image datasets.

London, ancestral home of the Anglos, may be the security camera capital of the world. It is estimated that "the average Londoner is caught on CCTV three hundred times a day," because they're everywhere. "There are now 691,000 CCTV cameras in London" (Ratcliffe 2022). That's more than enough material to piece together any citizen's movements, whether they've committed a crime or not. To capitalize on this latent surveillance potential, in 2021, the city of London bought "heaps of facial recognition tech" (Woodhams 2021). "The Met[ropolitan Police] will start using Retrospective Facial Recognition (RFR), as part of a £3 million, four-year deal with Japanese tech firm NEC," the same corporation servicing those Australian casinos. If the US is any example, London jumped the gun giving their police force unfettered access to these tools, which are so readily abused.

Later in 2021, nine schools in southwest Scotland said they would "start taking payments for school lunches by scanning the faces of pupils, claiming that the new system speeds up queues and is more Covid-secure than the card payments and fingerprint scanners they used previously" (O'Murchu 2021). While I'm all for bolstering public health, are we really to believe that initiatives like these are purely meant to increase safety and efficiency? A representative of Big Brother Watch, a watchdog group on data privacy, said this is "normalizing biometric identity checks for something that is mundane. You don't need to resort to airport style [technology] for children getting their lunch." We don't want the next generation to blindly accept that their faceprint will be collected at every point of sale just because that's what they grew up with. We have to draw the line somewhere. Modern tap-to-pay systems are plenty fast and hygienic enough.

Gratefully, we're entering a phase where enough folks have been harmed by facial recognition that regulators have begun to respond. For example, "the European Parliament has voted to back a total ban on biometric mass surveillance" (Lomas 2021).

Governments are starting to issue speeding tickets to companies like Clearview: They've "been fined almost $10 million by the UK's data protection watchdog for collecting the faces of UK citizens from the web and social media. The firm was also ordered to delete all of the data it holds on UK citizens," but who's to say if they actually dumped that data (Heikkilä 2022)? A ten-million-dollar fine equates to about 8 percent of the company's 2021 valuation. Far more work remains to bring facial recognition surveillance to heel, and that means pioneering new regulatory ground in collaboration with technology and ethics experts.

Massachusetts became the first US state to enact some semi-nuanced policies around facial recognition (rather than a blanket ban) in 2021. Previously, Massachusetts law enforcement agencies performed uninhibited photo identity lookups on the state's Registry of Motor Vehicles photo database with close to zero oversight. Thanks to the new restrictions, officials need "a court order before they can compare images to the database of photos and names held" in the state's various photo ID databases; now they "can't track someone in their personal life for personal reasons, like an ex-spouse, and so it prevents the most bald-faced types of potential misuse" (Peaslee 2021). Citizens and their representatives are split on whether these new restrictions go far enough. The ACLU of Massachusetts would have liked to see a full-blown warrant requirement. Why give cops more superpowers than they need, in an already overpoliced country?

People tend to think of privacy and safety as diametrically opposed, but that's an overly simplistic mental model fed to citizens from above. Kade Crockford, one of the most central figures in Massachusetts' push for common-sense facial recognition protections, said, "Technologies that advance our privacy also advance our safety. Think about fences, door locks, curtains on our windows, passwords, encryption software. All of these technologies simultaneously protect our privacy and our safety... Privacy is not the enemy of safety. It is its guarantor" (Crockford 2019). Facial recognition feels like a technology designed more like a gun than a screwdriver. Hence, let's be exceptionally careful as we find ways to use it—ways that increase our safety and convenience while simultaneously bolstering our privacy and freedom. It's entirely possible if we build systems together in public and include a diversity of folks in the conversation on regulation.

11

AI SNAKE OIL

Computer vision technology has another big problem, one it shares with AI more generally. It's too easy to sell.

If you're not getting your hands dirty tinkering with the latest open-source software tools, or at least reading (sober, non-sensational) journalism to keep current on the cutting edge of AI research, it's easy to lose a sense of what's feasible with AI and computer vision today. Folks get caught up in the echo chamber of hype around this bundle of sophisticated technologies, which has been marketed far and wide as a panacea to all of society's ills and inconveniences. It's remarkably easy to spend a shitload of money on AI snake oil—especially your corporate employer's money. Vicki Boykis, a machine learning expert, wrote, "We need to end the hype cycle around AI and ML pronto" (Boykis 2019).

Thankfully, Princeton Associate Professor Arvind Narayanan has been vocal about his notion that "for the process of science to work, we, as the public, must understand not just science but also pseudo-science" (Hulette 2021). Where real science demands an adherence to the scientific method, pseudo-science demands adherence to shareholder interests over reality.

In a world increasingly full of pseudo-science, it becomes much more difficult to extract signal from the noise.

Narayanan has been writing about and giving talks on "AI snake oil," which aptly describes a disappointing fraction of digital products and services on the market today. It's important to recognize it when you see it, and even more importantly, not to put more of it out into the world. So, what is it, and what does it look like?

FLAVORS OF SNAKE OIL

Overeager startups may throw around AI buzzwords to grow their fledgling businesses, even when machine learning isn't really central to their product. The "startup Engineer.ai says it uses artificial-intelligence technology to largely automate the development of mobile apps, but several current and former employees say the company exaggerates its AI capabilities to attract customers and investors" (Purnell 2019).

The company raised roughly thirty million dollars from a Softbank subsidiary, claiming that its human-assisted AI solution could help users create custom new software solutions in short order. However, insider sources "indicated that the company relies on human engineers in India and elsewhere to do most of that work, and that its AI claims are inflated even in light of the fake-it-till-you-make-it mentality common among tech startups" (Purnell 2019). Outsourcing to India doesn't count as automation.

We'll call this the *Wizard of Oz* (or perhaps "Elizabeth Holmes") version of AI snake oil. Behind the curtain, there's no magic. I fear this is but one glaring example in an iceberg of such companies, ones that piggyback off of the awe-inspiring effect that real scientific advancements in AI have had on the public in the last couple of decades. In fact, as of mid-2019, "nearly half of the companies in Europe that call themselves AI start-ups don't in fact use artificial intelligence" (Schulze 2019). MMC, a British VC firm, individually evaluated 2,830 European companies, which were classified as "AI" startups, and they found that only about 60 percent of those companies really incorporated some form of AI in their value proposition (Kelnar 2019). This is not to say that many companies are necessarily lying about their use of AI; they just aren't correcting anybody who says they're an AI company. That would be bad for business.

> "I think in most cases [startups] will be aware of how they're being classified," Kelnar added. But there is little incentive to correct a listing, since it spells potentially less investment down the line and it can pay to brand yourself as being an AI company. Startups that are labelled as being in the field of artificial intelligence attract fifteen to 50 percent more in their funding rounds than other technology startups (Olson 2019).

We'll call that snake oil by association. AI is hot right now, so if we pose as an AI company, the VC money will follow.

I love fancy new advancements in software. When they're unleashed unto the world, I want to play with them, get a handle on them, and put them on my résumé. When all you have is a hammer, everything starts to look like a nail. Likewise, when all you have is the ability to fine-tune an image classifier, everything starts to look like a potential computer-vision-powered software service. The sad truth for software nerds like me, however, is that often the simplest solution to a problem is the most elegant and best solution.

Computer vision is not simple. It's computationally expensive. For most purposes, AI is not the appropriate tool for the job. "AI" just happens to be where the marketing hype has really thrived in the first quarter of the twenty-first century. For example, if you want to count the number of people in a museum, you could train a computer vision algorithm to analyze security camera footage, classify what it sees as "human" or not, and total up the number of humans detected, or you could simply use turnstiles to count the number of people that come and go. Simpler is often better.

BULLSHIT AI

In his simultaneously wise and flippant treatise *On Bullshit*, American philosopher Harry G. Frankfurt presents a theory that bullshit is "intended to persuade without regard for truth. The liar cares about the truth and attempts to hide it; the bullshitter doesn't care if what they say is true or false, but cares only whether the listener is persuaded" (2005). Persuasion is important in sales. Bullshit has become prevalent in the AI industry because bullshit AI products can persuade customers to open their wallets just as effectively as empirically accurate, high-quality products do.

We say "snake oil" to mean bullshit products, but in the nineteenth century, some of the more honest traveling salesmen "may have peddled actual Chinese snake oil," which "contains

20 percent eicosapentaenoic acid (EPA), one of the two types of omega-3 fatty acids most readily used by our bodies" (Graber 2007). That's more omega-3s than salmon! It's not that snake oil never worked. The market was simply diluted with bull-shit knockoffs, giving the real thing a bad name. Rattlesnake oil, which lacked the same level of omega-3 content, was the first knockoff, followed by "snake oils" (only in name) con-taining nothing but modified mineral oil. The same problem has befallen AI and computer vision. The good stuff is out there for sale, but now you have to sift through mountains of bullshit to find it.

The most insidious flavor of AI snake oil may be the kind that actually technically uses some form of AI but in a poorly con-ceived way. Machine learning algorithms are garbage-in, gar-bage-out systems. You can only make reasonable predictions with AI if some predictive power is baked into the training data to begin with, which isn't always the case.

Take, for example, the often-cited Iris Flower dataset, intro-duced by the British statistician and biologist Ronald Fisher in 1936. Given just four important attributes—namely the lengths and widths of petals and sepals, in centimeters—from 150 observations of iris flowers, one can train a multi-class classification algorithm to distinguish with over 97 percent accuracy between three discrete classes of iris: the setosa, the versicolor, and the virginica.

Distinguishing between Iris types works surprisingly well, even with a fairly rudimentary classification algorithm, because the different classes of iris flowers actually tend to differ substantially in measurement. The setosa's petals are slimmer and shorter than the virginica's, with the versicolor's falling in between. The setosa also tends to have the widest sepals, making it easier to distinguish from the versicolor. We consider these distinctive measurements to be "predictive" input data for informing the "response" or "output" variable, namely the flower's species.

Rigorous, non-pseudo data science (just like the rest of science) starts with a plausible, refutable hypothesis, such as "iris species can be distinguished from one another by their measurable petal and sepal lengths and widths." This hypothesis is plausible because we've observed that different types of irises tend to have consistently different measurements. It's refutable because if we keep measuring more flowers and realize that the statistical correlation we found between species and their measurements was actually just a total coincidence, we can discard our flawed hypothesis.

With those criteria in mind, try your hand at evaluating this hypothesis: "A job candidate's suitability for an open role can be quantified by watching them talk for thirty seconds and evaluating their body language and speech patterns (ignoring the words they use)." Is this hypothesis plausible?

Actually, no. A candidate's suitability for the open position at your company is likely highly dependent on a number of complex factors, which cannot be discerned from their body language and speech patterns alone, certainly not within thirty seconds. What about their employment history, their educational background, or their portfolio of relevant projects? Isn't there some industry-specific metric by which your company might evaluate a prospective employee?

Nevertheless, the preposterous hypothesis above is what the startup 8andabove was built upon. They claimed to be able to take thirty-second video submissions from candidates and, leveraging the magic of computer vision, return scores quantifying their openness, enthusiasm, warmness, and kindness with breakdowns ranging from "adventurousness" to "intellect" ratings.

Narayanan said, "Millions of people applying for jobs have been subjected to these types of algorithmic assessment systems" (Hulette 2021). In a study evaluating eighteen "vendors of algorithmic pre-employment assessments (algorithms to screen candidates)," most were found to be opaque and potentially unlawful in new and interesting ways (Raghavan et al. 2019). It doesn't take a PhD in computer science to sort out that watching someone talk for thirty seconds won't yield accurate metrics about their emotional and intellectual IQ. Just because computer vision is a new and exciting field of technological research does not give it the ability to analyze data where data is absent.

This is a prime example of AI snake oil of the computer vision variety. The company was genuinely training deep-learning-based image analysis algorithms to make predictions based on visual input data. The outputs, however, were ultimately meaningless because the input data was never predictive. It simply can't be determined whether or not someone is fit for a job or how intelligent—and adventurous and kind and resourceful and sensitive—they are, based on a thirty-second video of them talking.

Since then, 8andabove has moved on, rebranding themselves as inclusive.hr, which provides "top organizations diversity and inclusion applications through insights and blockchain solutions." How a blockchain could be leveraged to help with corporate diversity and inclusion, or why that would be a good idea, is beyond me. For the snake oil salespeople at inclusive.hr, it's probably just another tech buzzword that opens wallets.

THE DANGERS

Smart people fall into the trap of opening their wallets for AI snake oil because they want something done quickly, they have corporate budget to burn, and a talented salesperson is actively trying to sell them on something that seems to work better than it actually works. It's often easier to outsource a project to a third-party vendor than it is to collaborate internally with the in-demand technical team within your organization.

Vendors of AI snake oil persist because they're more interested in profiting (and moving on to the next sucker) than in adding real value to the world. At best, they're unaware what they're selling is of low quality. If you hustle just a few slow-moving large enterprise clients who don't talk to one another, you can make off with a killing before word gets out that your brand of snake oil is just that.

AI snake oil is dangerous because it's expensive. Not only can it cost a lot to invest in a terrible AI system at the outset, but it can be a long time before you realize what you've purchased is bullshit. When you do finally realize the results you've been getting are essentially random, it can damage your ego—and even your brand's identity, if you're not careful. Rolling back the implementation can be time consuming and frustrating, and then you're left with the original problem you were trying to solve with AI.

SOME TIPS

How do you recognize AI snake oil before it's too late? Here are a few heuristics to deploy to this end.

Ask questions liberally. Often, we pay for things in order to bypass the need to think about them, to some extent. Resist the urge to spend money on computer vision products and services sight-unseen. Demand proof that the systems you're buying actually work. Inquire about the underlying mechanisms. Pry a little bit. How quickly do you encounter resistance? If you run into red tape ("sorry, that's proprietary") early on, take note and proceed with extreme caution. If a company is really doing something revolutionary, they won't need to keep it a secret from the world, because the competition won't be able to keep up regardless. Transparency is a hallmark of real innovation in AI.

Use common sense; *be skeptical.* A class at the University of Washington is titled "Calling Bullshit in the Age of Big Data." One of its professors pointed out that "you don't have to understand all the gears inside a black box in order to evaluate what you're being told" (Nijhuis 2017). Correlation does not amount to causation, but do the inputs and outputs seem *at least* plausibly correlated? If you tell me that your computer vision algorithm analyzes scans of horse retinas in order to make predictions about horse race outcomes, I will want to see proof. Even though the input data vaguely relates to horses, I'm skeptical that a horse's galloping speed has much to do with their retinal patterns. I'm always willing to be proven wrong, but that's exactly the sort of research paper where you need to be sure to peruse the "methodology" section.

Consider the scope of the solution you're considering buying. Does it solve one very specific problem very well, or does it claim to be able to solve dozens of various problems very well? I love a good fusion restaurant, but if the same restaurant claims to be able to make great hamburgers, tacos, sushi, gyros, borscht, pizza, and lo mein, I will wonder if any of their dishes are really any good. Favor products and services that claim to solve one niche problem very well over companies that claim their proprietary AI can run every aspect of your business for you.

Don't hand over enormous swaths of your data from the get-go. It's valuable stuff. If a vendor claims they'll need tons of historical data from your archives and a few months just to kickstart your collaboration, it's possible they're getting more out of the deal than you are. Be aware that data-hungry startups may use your data to train or fine-tune the same algorithms they repackage and resell to other clients. That said, it's impossible to start a data science project without at least some sample data, so your discretion is key.

Seek out the simplest solution to any problem first. Computer vision is an exciting new field, but if a problem can be solved more elegantly with a simpler tool, it probably should be. You don't get brownie points just for solving a solved problem with AI. Deep learning, for example, is typically computationally expensive and opaque, harder to explain and debug than writing a bunch of explicit rules.

Armed with curiosity, skepticism, common sense, and an Occam's-Razor approach to problem-solving, you should have an easier time navigating the high seas of bullshit AI. It shouldn't all have to be your responsibility, though. Regulators have to hold up their end of the deal and make it more difficult to take people's money without providing real value.

12

TAP THE BRAKES

Every race car needs a good set of brakes. Computer vision is a rocket ship with race car brakes. They need an upgrade.

In Silicon Valley parlance, every startup hopes to become "disruptive." *TechCrunch* even calls their annual startup event "Disrupt." To generate meaningful business and make a dent in the universe, entrepreneurs aim to smash the status quo. They tend to do so by diverting business from incumbent market leaders, by inviting users to adopt new (and hopefully better) tools or paradigms. Often, these sorts of "disruptions" are net positives for society, especially in the long run. However, technology companies on a quest to accumulate hordes of users as quickly as possible are more likely to get ahead of their skis—especially when there's little to zero legal precedent and, therefore, regulation in their domain. Facebook's old internal motto, "move fast and break things," became the title of a book subtitled "How Facebook, Google and Amazon Have Cornered Culture and Undermined Democracy." Let's not allow computer vision technologies to make such a bad name for themselves.

It's up to us as citizens and workers, both in and out of tech, to identify and neutralize the parts of new technologies that can and do cause us harm. We cannot kick back on autopilot, so to speak. We must have our foot on the brake pedal, ready to slow ourselves down when we begin to move too quickly over foggy new roads. We must not only break things that no longer serve us, but we must also hit the brakes when we're hurtling through established safeguards. Certain computer vision applications are already moving too fast and breaking things, kicking those who are already down and causing self-harm. We need to muster civic engagement around these issues to minimize potential future harm. News media and educational institutions will play key roles in this mobilization.

Uber disrupted the taxi industry. Airbnb disrupted the hotel industry. Now ride-sharing is cheaper, but the value of a taxi medallion (or a taxi driving permit) has collapsed entirely. Medallion owners, many of whom were immigrants who had invested their life savings or taken out massive loans, have since died by suicide, unable to cope with their financial ruin. I enjoy ride-sharing services just as much as the next millennial, but I wish we had done more to ease the transition for the affected parties.

Airbnb has more listings, globally, than the top five hotel brands combined. The New Orleans housing market, amongst others, has been decimated by well-to-do folks snatching up properties just to list them on Airbnb. That has made it impossible for longtime locals to stay afloat in their rental market. What's good for many may be catastrophic for some, but it doesn't have to be that way.

Disruption isn't just an edgy Silicon Valley buzzword. Disruption can be painful in real ways to real people, usually those on the margins, economically or otherwise. It takes sensible and proactive new regulatory policy to minimize destruction in the wake of technological disruption. Policy can't hope to move at the speed of tech, so it has to look ahead.

Successful entrepreneur Tim O'Reilly takes issue with Silicon Valley's obsession with rapid growth at all costs. LinkedIn cofounder Reid Hoffman and entrepreneur Chris Yeh published a book called *Blitzscaling,* in which they "argue that in today's world, it's essential to 'achieve massive scale at incredible speed' in order to seize the ground before competitors do. By their definition, blitzscaling (derived from the blitzkrieg or 'lightning war' strategy of Nazi general Heinz Guderian) 'prioritizes speed over efficiency,' and risks 'potentially disastrous defeat in order to maximize speed and surprise'" (O'Reilly 2019). Scaling fledgling companies and deploying revolutionary technologies at breakneck speed can cause considerable collateral damage as second-order effects are incurred without time for deliberation. It's entirely possible to start and grow a business in a steady, sustainable way that deliberately minimizes harm. O'Reilly has done so himself and recommends it over a "blitzscaling" approach.

Clearview AI is the most glaring example of a computer vision company actively choosing a blitzscaling approach. They collected at least twenty billion "faceprint" images from popular social media websites against each site's (essentially un-enforceable) terms of service. Our faceprints are "crucial to linking the digital data that's been accumulated about us with our identities in the real world. That is valuable not just to law enforcement but also to companies, advertisers, journalists," and more (Hill 2021). One lawyer likened this unwarranted collection of identity data to a hypothetical hairdresser who collects hair trimmings and sends them to a genetic testing lab for examination, building a database of their customers' personal information.

Clearview is paying a price for their wanton approach, but the toll may not be high enough. While "ten class-action complaints were filed against Clearview around the United States for invasion of privacy along with lawsuits from the ACLU and Vermont's attorney general," the company continues to develop lucrative contracts with non-law-enforcement third parties (Hill 2021). As of this writing, Clearview's valuation still sits in the hundreds of millions of dollars. In May of 2022, Clearview finally agreed "to limit its face database in the United States primarily to government agencies and not allow most American companies to have access to it" (Mac and Hill 2022). They're still facing heavy scrutiny in places like Greece and the EU, but they'll continue to grow as fast as they can wherever they're allowed to.

While implementing cut-and-dry bans on facial recognition isn't an outrageous gut reaction to this towering wave of technological encroachment, it will prove too simplistic in the long run. I spoke with AI ethics expert Dahlia Peterson at Georgetown's Center for Security and Emerging Technology (CSET), who recognizes that facial recognition promises hard-to-ignore potential for good, such as the ability to catch sex abusers. However, in practice, she said, "You don't necessarily want these technologies to become more accurate and then widely used without any controls. That could easily lead to intensified policing in already over-policed populations." She said:

In terms of facial recognition, it pretty much removes the ability for you to have any meaningful expectation of privacy. You are completely unaware most of the time when the technology is being deployed, and where or how it may be used to make decisions on your civil liberties, especially if you are a person of color... If you are a black woman, for example. The technology can still be very inaccurate on minorities and people of color.

That said, law enforcement agencies hold massive sway in the US, and Peterson said, "The ship has sailed on facial recognition." She believes that at the very least, "there should be warrant requirements for running facial recognition on people who are very clearly suspected of committing a crime. That has to be combined with what they're already doing in Europe under the GDPR, which is... implementing automated face pixelation." What is that?

Automated face pixelation is the idea that your face should remain unidentifiable in any camera feeds of public places—until someone has committed a crime in that particular area. Peterson said at that point, "the police [have to] obtain a warrant to de-anonymize that individual and actually be able to identify them." Slightly more nuanced policies like this one strike a healthy balance, maintaining most people's anonymity in most situations while unlocking the potential to leverage computer vision for justice where justice is needed. It's not foolproof, but it's progress.

While companies like Clearview shift their focus to government agencies and enterprise clients, a mysterious company called PimEyes has stepped into the public spotlight, and it smells like stalker-ware. Kashmir Hill invites us to "imagine what you would do with a face-identifying app on your phone: a Shazam for people. You would never forget someone's name at a party again" (2021). Unfortunately, it also means that if you have a former life you'd prefer to forget, any paying PimEyes user will be able to photograph you—say, at a bar, or in the park—and dredge up images that you'd prefer to keep in the past, revealing more about your identity than you might have cared to divulge to a stranger on the street. How will we decide and enforce whether or not services like these are allowed to continue to exist and operate?

Watchdog organizations like the Technology for Liberty Program at the ACLU of Massachusetts use our "unprecedented access to information and communication to protect and enrich open society and individual rights by implementing basic reforms to ensure our new tools do not create inescapable digital cages" (ACLU 2021). The program's director Kade Crockford works to ensure that "privacy and civil liberties law keeps pace with new technologies, with a focus on how systems of surveillance and control impact not just the society in general but their primary targets—people of color, Muslims, immigrants, and dissidents."

Their biography essentially contains the checklist, as far as effective actions one can take to help society steer away from dystopia: writing, researching, organizing, lobbying, and advocacy. We have to look to folks like Crockford for leadership and put them in front of broader audiences while supplying them with hard resources they need to exert their influence.

To help dodge the worst-case societal side effects of mature computer vision, we have to curb domestic law enforcement use of facial recognition, implementing policies that at least require agencies to procure warrants to access faceprint data from surveillance camera feeds.

We need to generate more balanced, better-curated image data-sets for training large computer vision models, doing our best to avoid amplifying harmful cultural biases. A vision model shouldn't be more likely to classify someone as a woman just because they're in a kitchen cooking or cleaning. Skin cancer detection algorithms should be available for more than just white people. We can boycott systems that fail to serve one type of person and not another based on protected traits like gender and religion.

Exercise ample skepticism around physiognomy. You can't know if someone will commit another crime based on their facial landmarks. You can't know just by watching a video clip of someone's face whether or not they'll be good at some job. Neither can a computer. The predictive data does not exist in the relationship between our eyes, noses, and mouths.

Peterson implores policymakers to "work with people who have a very firm technical background, to be able to get a sense of how the technologies are actually designed, and if they are flawed by design." It's too easy to get excited about something that claims to work well without looking under the hood. Maybe it works "well" for all the wrong reasons. We can't turn a blind eye to the underlying mechanisms just because they give the sort of results we were hoping for.

Engineers and researchers have to flock in the direction of transparent, explainable computer vision systems so that when these systems make important decisions, those decisions can be justified. Opaque systems can easily become quietly racist or misogynist, for example, and that danger is magnified when they score seductively well on overly simplistic or perverse target metrics. The sacrifice in predictive power is usually worth it for explainability, and explainable models are improving all the time, frequently outperforming the previous year's black-box methods.

We have to stop exporting computer hardware to places where it'll be used for evil, like penal colonies in Xinjiang. Peterson points out that "China's AI surveillance ecosystem cannot be divorced from the fact that it is very much supported by Western technology, including major US companies Intel and Xilinx. Their chips are very clearly indicated by Chinese public security services as required or necessary equipment. China does not currently have the ability to design their own alternatives, although they are trying really hard."

Last but not least, we must keep the discourse around computer vision, and what its proliferation means for us all, active and inclusive. Peterson underscored that "it's especially important to have civil society and the media putting these technologies into context, explaining how they are being used and how they affect human rights." Investigative journalists like Kashmir Hill, think tanks like CSET, and humanitarian organizations like Human Rights Watch could use more of our time, attention, or donations. Bolstering that whole class of institutions gives us the ability to slow down to a sane pace when technologies like generative art come crashing through the wall to threaten the livelihoods of comic artists and partially autonomous vehicles begin taking more lives.

CONCLUSION

Visualize May in the year 2037. The temperature is seventy-eight degrees Fahrenheit in balmy Buffalo, New York, which has experienced a population swell as winters became milder here while summers at lower latitudes became sweatier, smokier, wetter, and generally less livable. You're glad you decided to move here when you did, before rent prices got out of control. You tie your shoes, slide on your glasses, and summon a ride to the clinic. It's time for a little visit with the radiologist.

Just as you reach the bottom of your morning coffee, a small icon gently pulses on your left-side eyeglass lens to let you know your lift will arrive momentarily. You head outside. As you look down the street, your glasses read the license plate number of the approaching minivan. They draw a yellow border with a label around the vehicle. Confirmed: That's your ride.

Your usual favorite spot, the front-left seat, which used to be known as the "driver's seat," is occupied by an eight-year-old with a lap full of breakfast burrito. Her mother sits to her right, filling out a field trip liability waiver or something. You make pleasant small talk for part of the ride. After they've been dropped off at school, the car stops for a yellow light near the hospital. Hoping to exit early and walk the last half-block, you tug on the door latch. The robo-taxi politely requests that you please wait until it has cleared this common ambulance path before disembarking. You're tempted to manually override it, but just then the light turns green and your car slides into the outpatient drop-off zone—just as a self-driving ambulance comes screaming out from behind you, successfully delivering a stroke patient to the ER, just in time. You leave no tip. None is called for.

The radiologist is pleased to inform you that you will not, in fact, require a PET scan today. Thanks to recent algorithmic advances in medical image processing, a regular CT scan will suffice. This downgrade spares you from the same amount of radiation that people are exposed to naturally over the course of about five years. Immediately after the imaging session, you review your results with the technician in the next room. The algorithmic classifier turned up some promising preliminary results, but you'll get an email in a few hours after the doctor has had a chance to sign off on the analysis.

Universal basic income has most of your bare necessities covered, but you've still been applying for a new full-time job because you hope to own your own home before you're sixty-five. In the meantime, you've been supplementing your income by killing two birds with one stone—watching as-yet unreleased movies (that you'll probably want to see eventually anyway) and getting paid for it. You walk through the park to the local cineplex, where one of the theaters has been equipped to handle test screenings. Along your stroll, a magnificent bird of prey circles above the park. Curious, you tap a certain area on your spectacle frames and maintain your gaze on the aerial predator. Turns out it's actually an adolescent bald eagle, not a red-tailed hawk!

The test-screening company has your faceprint and baseline emotive expressions on file, but they're contractually bound to keep that data under lock and key into perpetuity. You sit down for the latest installment in a perhaps overextended superhero franchise. Behind the movie screen, infrared cameras take note of your laughs, gasps, eyebrow raises, eye rolls, and bathroom breaks, aggregating the whole audience's reactions into time-series metrics.

Later, the film's producers, director, and editor will use these scores as they decide which scenes to milk for more laughs, and which to cut entirely. As the credits roll and you make your way for the exit, you wonder, on a whim: How many seats are in here? You tap your glasses, ask the question out loud, and direct your gaze back at the sea of red velvet seats. It takes a second. Turns out it's exactly 250 seats. Curiosity satisfied.

Earlier, you typed up a little shopping list to knock out on the return voyage. You walk a little out of your way to the smart-market, which you prefer over other grocery stores nearby. In the global foods section, you can't recall which container of soy sauce is the one with too much sodium. Your glasses translate the Japanese text on the bottle into English in real-time. It was the one with the green cap. You wonder if conveniences like these will help reduce the cumulative number of trips you will have to make to the hospital in your lifetime, or if that's just wishful thinking.

On the walk back home, you pass by the traffic intersection where all the news vans were stationed last week. After a traffic camera triggered a confident face match with a photo from the missing persons database, the police were able to pull the kidnapper's license plate number and surprise them at home. Now that fourteen-year-old girl is back with her family, and the perpetrator's criminal career is over.

Today was a good day.

Developments in computer vision research and development, spurred by academic curiosity, capitalism, and national security initiatives have already reshaped society around us. They will only continue to do so, to the point where computer vision becomes a ubiquitous, if not obvious, element of our day-to-day lives.

Giving computers the ability to "see" the world around them, and make judgments and decisions based on what they see, unlocks mountains of potential for positive utility. It also opens a moral and ethical can of worms, casting us into uncharted waters where the new rules will have to be made up as people get hurt. The march of science and technology never stops. The question is just how quickly we can bring a greater diversity of folks into the conversation to help computer vision tools work equitably across all walks of life.

People should be genuinely excited about the ways in which computer vision can help without throwing caution to the wind. As with any new tool, computer vision-powered tools should be adequately understood, vetted, and benchmarked before we hope to rely on them. This is especially true in critical applications like medicine and law enforcement.

Historically, policy has been more reactive than proactive, moving slower than entrepreneurship. Therefore, policymakers should be working closely with think tanks, computer vision researchers, and engineers to navigate the new moral landscape introduced by the exponential maturation of computer vision technology.

In the same way that nuclear disasters have cast a negative light on fission as a reliable source of energy, early accidents involving self-driving cars, over-policing with facial recognition, and algorithm-based medical misdiagnoses will make people wonder if computer vision is really the right tool for some of these jobs. However, once we get appropriate guardrails in place, self-driving cars will operate more reliably than human drivers, law enforcement agencies won't be allowed to identify you in surveillance footage without a warrant, and accurate diagnostic tools will ease the burden on sagging health care systems.

Early attempts at what came to be known as computer vision go back to at least the '60s, so it's incredibly exciting to witness the inflection point we've reached some sixty years later. Cheaper state-of-the-art computer hardware, bigger datasets, and cutting-edge algorithmic theory have converged to give legs to today's computer vision renaissance.

The prospect of ubiquitous self-driving cars inches nearer with every advance in computer vision. Imagine a world where there's far less road traffic because taking many robo-taxi rides has become markedly more affordable than owning and maintaining a personal vehicle.

If you really must have one of your own, you can apply for a permit to send it off to ferry people about while you're not using it, earning a passive income and eliminating the need for parking spots at the office and at home. Private parking lots will become economically unviable. Highways will be safer when drunk, sleepy, and otherwise reckless drivers are displaced by rule-abiding algorithmic ones. Forget cars, though. Hopefully, eventually, those same highways will just give way to public transit infrastructure and green space.

Generative vision models will empower creators. Swaths of people with essentially zero drawing or digital painting skills will be able to type out descriptions of stuff they want illustrated, and generative art tools will create "original" artwork for them. There will be no shortage of ways to make a living as a talented, creative individual just because more is possible with automation.

Video editors and digital animators will have more assistance to automate boring tasks and focus on the truly creative elements of their jobs. A new wave of entrepreneurs will experience a gold rush as it becomes easier to develop new computer vision tools for niche applications—without even knowing how to code, necessarily—in fields as diverse as oceanography, filmmaking, and plumbing.

Shopping and entertainment will be transformed. Your (perhaps nonprescription) glasses will be able to read sports jersey numbers off of the field, superimposing player performance stats as you wish. It may feel a little dystopian to some when real-time ads and discounts pop up as you walk through the shopping mall, a la *Minority Report*, but commensurate conveniences will balance out the experience.

Many vision-centric jobs will be displaced by computer vision systems, so it would be in our best interest to start preparing graceful transition strategies for those whose jobs will be automated first. That's probably going to look more like subsidized vocational training programs than hard bans on computer vision applications.

Snake-oil salespeople will run amok, shilling computer vision solutions that either don't perform as well as they claim to, don't actually use computer vision at all, use it in a way that damages society, or uses it in a context where much simpler solutions would work just as well. Let's do our best to oust those frauds as quickly as we spot them so that a useful suite of technologies doesn't get an unnecessarily bad reputation.

We need to demystify computer vision and other branches of AI research for the masses and especially for lawmakers. Research will need to move in the direction of explainability and an education-forward approach. It will be incumbent on toolmakers to ask: Does what I've created more closely resemble a screwdriver or a gun? How can the computer vision applications I've designed be abused by those wishing ill upon others, and how can I prevent that?

The greater the number and variety of people who know about computer vision and what it could mean for our global society, the better off future generations will be.

ACKNOWLEDGMENTS

Three thousand thanks to this book's interview subjects. It was lovely chatting with each of you. If any deep or lasting insights are to be found here, thank you for lending them. Please let me keep believing you would have picked up the phone even if I hadn't opened with "I'm writing a book about [insert your passion and specialty here]."

Catherine: Thank you for your selfless love and support. You've kept me sane and surrounded by plants for almost four years—through a pandemic, a roach-infested apartment, and turbulence at work. I love and admire you. Today you fed me chickpea stew. I'll bake you a pizza later this week. Let's go dancing.

To my family: Thank you for having my back. I will always have yours.

Michael, Zach: Thank you for the treasure of your sterling friendship and for pushing me. To the valued members of the formidable Prospect Park Chess club: I will see you on Wednesday night, at the usual spot. Please chess to impress.

I tip my hat to Kashmir Hill, Eric Topol, and the rest of the hard-working authors and journalists whose grueling labor has been repackaged here. Please keep bringing that Promethean fire down to the people. It is much appreciated.

This work would have suffered without critiques from Alexander Pyles, Cameron Alexander, Pavita Singh, Kenneth Cain, Zach Kuperstein, Amanda Brown, Ben T. Elliott, and others. Thank you for your time, attention, and discernment. Thanks to John Chancey and Michelle Pollack for helping me get this onto some shelves.

To Eric Koester, the Manuscripts Modern Author Accelerator, and Manuscripts, LLC: You provide the tools, structure, and community required to start and finish one's first-ever book writing and publishing journey. You had to know that some of it would end up like this. Thanks anyhow. I'll be encouraging more folks to enroll in the program to push their unique stories out into the universe.

An extra special shout-out to my author community, the faithful few who preordered a copy as soon as I had a first draft in hand. You helped me pay the pros who actually knew what they were doing and charged me for it. Here's that book I owed you, and you're in it:

Joe Alexander-Short	Dante Bertana*
Pablo Anzoategui	Kevin Bitter
Beth Avon	Catherine Borst
Adam Becker	Pete Boscacci
Emma Bernstein	Mark and Frances Boscacci*

Christopher Boscacci

Larry Brown

Joyce and Leo Burns

Alejandra Cantú

Jaime Cheng

Chris Chung

Julie Craig

Sabina Del Rosso

Jaime Delgado Cultrera

Miranda Di Biase

Kira Dineen

Sachit Egan

Anthony Festa

Mary Foran

Peter Geiger

Frazer Goldberg

Leah Gordon

Brian Grau

Zach Gryder

Ryan Hamelin

Sam Heath

Robert Hillery

Ariel Jankelowitz

Mitchell Kain

Keith Kennedy

Marc Khuri-Yakub

Eric Koester

Dilyan Kovachev

Zach Kuperstein

Mary Legallet*

Bruce Li

Yish Lim

Dr. Tintina Pereira

Michael Mansour

Marius Matioc

Catherine Mayo

Owen McInnis

Shane McLeod

Trey Miller

Michael Mullen

Colin Muller

Samira Munir

Bryce Murphy

Rommel Nabayan

Ali Nelson

Andrew Noonan

James O'Shaughnessy

Victor Oliveira

Lorena Pereira

Tomas Pereira

Juan Carlos Pereira

Matt Pritchett

Daniel Quackenbush

Mimy Regjo

Kristo Regjo

Allison Romero

William Ross

Erika Russi

Malik Salam

Athena Scruton Lathos

Nicholas Shen

Denise Streckert

Erika Svensson

Winson Tam

David Vazquez

Orion Wilson

* Exceedingly generous supporter

APPENDIX

INTRODUCTION

Lynch, Shana. 2022. "The State of AI in 9 Charts." *Stanford University Human-Centered Artificial Intelligence* (blog). March 16, 2022. https://hai.stanford.edu/news/state-ai-9-charts.

US Department of Energy. 2019. "The Ultimate Fast Facts Guide to Nuclear Energy." January 16, 2019. https://stage.energy.gov/ne/articles/ultimate-fast-facts-guide-nuclear-energy.

01: I SEE YOU

Arastey, Guillermo Martinez. 2020. "Computer Vision in Sport." *Sport Performance Analysis*, April 17, 2020. https://www.sportperformanceanalysis.com/article/computer-vision-in-sport.

American Civil Liberties Union. 2022. "Automatic License Plate Readers." February 15, 2022. https://www.aclu.org/issues/privacy-technology/location-tracking/automatic-license-plate-readers.

Chadwick, Jonathan. 2022. "Apple Lets You Use Face ID to Unlock Your iPhone When Wearing a Mask." *Daily Mail Online,* February 8, 2022. https://www.dailymail.co.uk/sciencetech/article-10452615/Apple-lets-use-Face-ID-unlock-iPhone-wearing-MASK.html.

Cirad-France. 2013. "PlantNet." Apple App Store. February 15, 2013. https://apps.apple.com/us/app/plantnet/id600547573.

Cornell Lab of Ornithology. 2023. "Merlin Bird ID." Google Play Store. February 3, 2023. https://play.google.com/store/apps/details?id=com.labs.merlinbirdid.app.

Dean, Brian. 2021. "iPhone Users and Sales Stats for 2022." *Backlinko,* May 28, 2021. https://backlinko.com/iphone-users.

Gu, Xinxing. 2019. "Google Translate's Instant Camera Translation Gets an Upgrade." *Google Translate* (blog). July 10, 2019. https://blog.google/products/translate/google-translates-instant-camera-translation-gets-upgrade/.

Kanet, John, and Prince Kohli. 2021. "ADAS Analysis Creates Path for Auto Insurance Rating." Lexis Nexis Risk Solutions. November 9, 2021. https://lexisnexis.turtl.co/story/multivariate-adas-whitepaper/.

New York City Department of Transportation. 2021. "Bicyclist Ridership Statistics and Reports." August 29, 2022. https://www.nyc.gov/html/dot/html/bicyclists/bikestats.shtml#crashdata.

Parks Associates. 2019. "Significant Change in Rates for Installation Methods Indicates DIY Is on the Rise." *Parks Associates* (blog). May 24, 2019. https://www.parksassociates.com/blog/article/pr-05242019.

Tuohy, Jennifer Pattison. 2021. "Ring Video Doorbells Are Finally Getting Package Alerts." *The Verge,* September 28, 2021. https://www.theverge.com/2021/9/28/22691923/ring-video-doorbell-package-alerts-amazon-event.

Wilson, Cecilia, Charlene Willis, Joan K Hendrikz, Robyne Le Brocque, and Nicholas Bellamy. 2010. "Speed Cameras for the Prevention of Road Traffic Injuries and Deaths." *Cochrane Database of Systematic Reviews,* October 6, 2010. https://doi.org/10.1002/14651858.cd004607.pub4.

Wise, Jason. 2022. "40 Smartphone Statistics 2023: How Many People Have Smartphones?" *EarthWeb,* December 28, 2022. https://earthweb.com/smartphone-statistics/.

02: SUMMER VISION PROJECT

Cukierski, Will. 2013. "Dogs vs. Cats." Kaggle. Microsoft Research, September 25, 2013. https://www.kaggle.com/competitions/dogs-vs-cats/overview.

Green, Jennifer, Anna Doble, and Jules Bartl. 2019. "How a Kingfisher Helped Reshape Japan's Bullet Train." *BBC News,* March 26, 2019. https://www.bbc.com/news/av/science-environment-47673287.

JFK Library. 2019. "Address at Rice University, September 12, 1962 (USG 15 29)." June 28, 2019. 18:46. https://www.youtube.com/watch?v=iiC-E8vl7Fw

Papert, Seymour. 1966. "The Summer Vision Project." Massachusetts Institute of Technology, August 1, 1966. https://dspace.mit.edu/handle/1721.1/6125.

03: MOTHERBOARDS AGAINST DRUNK DRIVING

Bachman, Elon, and @icapulet (Twitter). 2022. "Digital Record of Tesla Crashes Resulting in Death." Tesla Deaths. December 25, 2022. https://www.tesladeaths.com/.

Barry, Keith. 2021. "Most New Cars Have Safety Technology That Prevents Crashes, Report Shows." *Consumer Reports,* December 18, 2021. https://www.consumerreports.org/car-safety/most-new-cars-have-aeb-safety-tech-that-prevents-crashes-a4660106723/.

Bertoncello, Michele, and Dominik Wee. 2015. "Ten Ways Autonomous Driving Could Redefine the Automotive World." *McKinsey & Company* (blog). June 1, 2015. https://www.mckinsey.com/industries/automotive-and-assembly/our-insights/ten-ways-autonomous-driving-could-redefine-the-automotive-world.

Brekke, Dan. 2019. "Anthony Levandowski: 'Going All the Way' and the Lessons of Real Mistakes." *KQED,* September 4, 2019. https://www.kqed.org/news/11770687/anthony-levandowski-google-waymo-uber-pronto-cross-country-drive.

comma.ai. 2022. "Openpilot." Accessed March 3, 2023. https://comma.ai/openpilot.

Hotz, George. 2020. "Openpilot GitHub Readme." GitHub. Comma.ai, January 17, 2020. https://github.com/commaai/openpilot.

Krisher, Tom. 2021. "Feds Probe NY Tesla Crash That Killed Man Changing Flat Tire." *AP News,* September 3, 2021. https://apnews.com/article/technology-business-6127ae797c528ca1d5322efc43439a12.

National Highway Traffic Safety Administration. 2008. "National Motor Vehicle Crash Causation Study." July 1, 2008. https://highways.dot.gov/safety/data-analysis-tools/rsdp/rsdp-tools/national-motor-vehicle-crash-causation-study-nmvccs.

O'Kane, Sean. 2021. "Apple Reportedly Wants to Launch a Self-Driving EV in 2025 with a Custom Chip." *The Verge,* November 18, 2021. https://www.theverge.com/2021/11/18/22789615/apple-self-driving-car-project-titan-custom-processor-ev.

Rao, Venkatesh. 2015. "Getting Reoriented." *Breaking Smart* (blog). August 10, 2015. https://breakingsmart.com/en/season-1/getting-reoriented/.

SAE International. 2021. "Taxonomy and Definitions for Terms Related to Driving Automation Systems for On-Road Motor Vehicles." April 30, 2021. https://www.sae.org/standards/content/j3016_202104.

Tesla, Inc. 2023. "Autopilot." Accessed January 29, 2023. https://www.tesla.com/autopilot.

US Congress. 2021. House. *Investing in a New Vision for the Environment and Surface Transportation in America Act.* HR 3684. 117th Cong., 1st sess. Introduced in House June 4, 2021.
https://www.govinfo.gov/app/details/BILLS-117hr3684ih.

Vanderwerp, Dave. 2020. "Is a $1000 Aftermarket Add-on as Capable as Tesla's Autopilot and Cadillac's Super Cruise?" *Car and Driver,* February 10, 2020.
https://www.caranddriver.com/features/a30341053/self-driving-technology-comparison/.

Wakabayashi, Daisuke. 2018. "Self-Driving Uber Car Kills Pedestrian in Arizona, Where Robots Roam." *The New York Times,* March 19, 2018.
https://www.nytimes.com/2018/03/19/technology/uber-driverless-fatality.html.

World Health Organization. 2018. "Global Status Report on Road Safety 2018." December 7, 2018. Geneva, Switzerland.
https://apps.who.int/iris/handle/10665/276462.

04: IN SILICO

American Cancer Society. 2018. "Understanding Radiation Risk from Imaging Tests." August 3, 2018.
https://www.cancer.org/treatment/understanding-your-diagnosis/tests/understanding-radiation-risk-from-imaging-tests.html.

Arcas, Blaise Agüera y, Alexander Todorov, and Margaret Mitchell. 2018. "Do Algorithms Reveal Sexual Orientation or Just Expose Our Stereotypes?" *Blaise Aguera y Arcas* (blog), *Medium.* January 18, 2018.
https://medium.com/@blaisea/do-algorithms-reveal-sexual-orientation-or-just-expose-our-stereotypes-d998fafdf477.

Bryan, R. Nick. 2016. "Look Ahead—Machine Learning in Radiology." *Radiological Society of North America,* May 1, 2016.
https://web.archive.org/web/20160502114237/
http://www.rsna.org/News.aspx?id=19018.

Centers for Disease Control and Prevention. 2022. "Health Insurance Portability and Accountability Act of 1996 (HIPAA)." June 27, 2022.
https://www.cdc.gov/phlp/publications/topic/hipaa.html.

Murphy, Heather. 2017. "Why Stanford Researchers Tried to Create a 'Gaydar' Machine." *The New York Times,* October 9, 2017.
https://www.nytimes.com/2017/10/09/science/stanford-sexual-orientation-study.html.

Recht, Michael, and R. Nick Bryan. 2017. "Artificial Intelligence: Threat or Boon to Radiologists?" *Journal of the American College of Radiology* 14, no. 11 (August): 1476–80.
https://doi.org/10.1016/j.jacr.2017.07.007.

Tingley, Kim. 2018. "Trying to Put a Value on the Doctor-Patient Relationship."
The New York Times, May 16, 2018.
https://www.nytimes.com/interactive/2018/05/16/magazine/health-issue-
reinvention-of-primary-care-delivery.html.

Topol, Eric J. 2019. *Deep Medicine: How Artificial Intelligence Can Make
Healthcare Human Again.* New York: Basic books.

Wang, Yilun, and Michal Kosinski. 2018. "Deep Neural Networks Are More
Accurate than Humans at Detecting Sexual Orientation from Facial Images."
Journal of Personality and Social Psychology 114, no. 2: 246–57.
https://doi.org/10.1037/pspa0000098.

05: YOUR OWN WORST CRITIC

Fawaz, Ather. 2021. "OpenAI's Diffusion Models Beat GANs at What They Do
Best." *Neowin,* May 16, 2021.
https://www.neowin.net/news/openais-diffusion-models-beat-gans-at-what-
they-do-best/.

Gault, Matthew. 2022. "An AI-Generated Artwork Won First Place at a State
Fair Fine Arts Competition, and Artists Are Pissed." *Vice,* August 31, 2022.
https://www.vice.com/en/article/bvmvqm/an-ai-generated-artwork-won-
first-place-at-a-state-fair-fine-arts-competition-and-artists-are-pissed.

Mallonee, Laura. 2018. "Auschwitz Photographs Hidden from the Nazis Are
Given New Life in Color." *Artsy* (blog). November 26, 2018.
https://www.artsy.net/article/artsy-editorial-auschwitz-photographs-hidden-
nazis-new-life-color.

Pennington, Clarke. 2023. "Generative AI: The New Frontier for VC
Investment." *Forbes,* January 18, 2023.
https://www.forbes.com/sites/columbiabusinessschool/2023/01/17/
generative-ai-the-new-frontier-for-vc-investment/?sh=590a8bd5519c.

06: AN EYE FOR TALENT

Adobe Inc. 2023. "Adobe Sensei Powers Creative Cloud." Creative Cloud
Artificial Intelligence. Accessed March 1, 2023.
https://www.adobe.com/sensei/creative-cloud-artificial-intelligence.html.

Edwards, Tom. 2023. "Tom Edwards Awards & Recommendations."
BlackFin360 (blog). January 11, 2023.
https://blackfin360.com/tom-edwards-recommendations/.

Google. 2023. "Google Glass Case Studies." *Google* (blog). Accessed February 27, 2023.
https://www.google.com/glass/case-studies/#dhl.

Hallman, Jessica. 2022. "Machine Learning Model Could Better Measure
Baseball Players' Performance." *ScienceDaily,* April 6, 2022.
https://www.sciencedaily.com/releases/2022/04/220406101805.htm.

Heaton, Connor, and Prasenjit Mitra. 2022. "Using Machine Learning to Describe How Players Impact the Game in the MLB." MIT Sloan Sports Analytics Conference, March 4, 2022. https://www.sloansportsconference.com/research-papers/using-machine-learning-to-describe-how-players-impact-the-game-in-the-mlb.

Perkins, Robert. 2017. "Neural Networks Model Audience Reactions to Movies." *California Institute of Technology* (blog). July 21, 2017. https://www.caltech.edu/about/news/neural-networks-model-audience-reactions-movies-79098.

Phillips, Gene D. 2005. *Godfather: The Intimate Francis Ford Coppola*. Lexington: University Press of Kentucky.

Savvides, Lexy. 2015. "Adobe's Morph Cut Is Like Autotune for Videos." *CNET,* June 22, 2015. https://www.cnet.com/tech/services-and-software/adobes-morph-cut-is-like-autotune-for-videos/.

Wear, Matthew, Ryan Beal, Tim Matthews, Tim Norman, and Sarvapali Ramchurn. 2022. "Learning from the Pros: Extracting Professional Goalkeeper Technique from Broadcast Footage." Cornell University, February 22, 2022. https://arxiv.org/abs/2202.12259v1.

Willens, Michele. 2000. "Putting Films to the Test, Every Time." *The New York Times,* June 25, 2000. https://www.nytimes.com/2000/06/25/movies/film-putting-films-to-the-test-every-time.html.

Yue, Yisong, and Rose Houghton. 2017. "New Technology Watches You While You Watch Movies." *ABC Radio National*, July 27, 2017. https://www.abc.net.au/radionational/programs/drive/facial-recognition/8749962.

07: NEMATODE BRAINS

Wachowski, Lana, and Lilly Wachowski. 1999. *The Matrix*. United States: Warner Bros.

08: SCREWDRIVERS VERSUS GUNS

Allyn, Bobby. 2022. "Deepfake Video of Zelenskyy Could Be 'Tip of the Iceberg' in Info War, Experts Warn." *NPR*, March 17, 2022. https://www.npr.org/2022/03/16/1087062648/deepfake-video-zelenskyy-experts-war-manipulation-ukraine-russia.

Cook, Jesselyn. 2021. "Selfies, Surgeries and Self-Loathing: Inside the Facetune Epidemic." *HuffPost*, June 4, 2021. https://www.huffpost.com/entry/facetune-selfies-surgeries-body-dysmorphia_n_60926a11e4b0b9042d989d48.

Nelson, Randy. 2018. "These Apps and Games Have Spent the Most Time at No. 1 on the App Store." *Sensor Tower,* July 2018.
https://sensortower.com/blog/number-one-apps.

O'Sullivan, Donie. 2023. "Nonconsensual Deepfake Porn Puts AI in Spotlight." *CNN,* February 16, 2023.
https://www.cnn.com/2023/02/16/tech/nonconsensual-deepfake-porn/index.html.

Perez, Sarah. 2021. "Facetune Maker Lightricks Raises $130 Million Ahead of M&A Plans." *TechCrunch,* September 20, 2021.
https://techcrunch.com/2021/09/20/facetune-maker-lightricks-raises-130-million-ahead-of-ma-plans/.

Revosoft Technologies. 2019. "Skin Tone Booth." Apple App Store. December 30, 2019.
https://apps.apple.com/us/app/skin-tone-booth-face-body/id1491849161.

Spina, Ellie. 2021. "'Blackface Vibes': Fans Accuse Khloé Kardashian of 'Blackfishing' in Recent Instagram Post." *Yahoo!,* June 18, 2021.
https://www.yahoo.com/lifestyle/fans-accuse-khloe-kardashian-blackfishing-recent-instagram-160009010.html.

Wells, Georgia, Jeff Horwitz, and Deepa Seetharaman. 2021. "Facebook Knows Instagram Is Toxic for Teen Girls, Company Documents Show." *The Wall Street Journal,* September 14, 2021.
https://www.wsj.com/articles/facebook-knows-instagram-is-toxic-for-teen-girls-company-documents-show-11631620739?mod=article_inline.

Witness Media Lab. 2022. "Prepare, Don't Panic: Synthetic Media and Deepfakes." July 25, 2022.
https://lab.witness.org/projects/synthetic-media-and-deep-fakes/.

09: LUDDITES AND TROGLODYTES

Aristotle. 2017. *Politics.* Translated by Benjamin Jowett. Digireads.com Publishing.

Blaug, Mark. 1997. *Economic Theory in Retrospects.* Cambridge, United Kingdom: Cambridge University Press.

Conniff, Richard. 2011. "What the Luddites Really Fought Against." *Smithsonian Magazine*, March 1, 2011.
https://www.smithsonianmag.com/history/what-the-luddites-really-fought-against-264412/.

Dunleavy, Jerry. 2021. "US Warns about Doing Business in Xinjiang amid Uyghur Genocide." *Washington Examiner*, July 13, 2021.
https://www.washingtonexaminer.com/news/us-warns-business-xinjiang-uyghur-genocide.

Gandhi, Mahatma. 2023. "The Place of Machinery." Gandhian Institutions: Bombay Sarvodaya Mandal & Gandhi Research Foundation. Accessed February 24, 2023.
https://www.mkgandhi.org/voiceoftruth/machinery.htm.

Kirby, Jen. 2020. "Concentration Camps and Forced Labor: China's Repression of the Uighurs, Explained." *Vox*, July 28, 2020. https://www.vox.com/2020/7/28/21333345/uighurs-china-internment-camps-forced-labor-xinjiang.

Lemar, Paula. 2021. "Lyft Statistics—Lyft's Revenue, Number of Users & Marketshare." *The Rideshare Guy Blog and Podcast* (blog). January 22, 2021. https://therideshareguy.com/lyft-statistics/.

Lemar, Paula. 2022. "Uber Passenger & Driver Statistics, Demographics, Revenue, & More." *The Rideshare Guy Blog and Podcast* (blog). July 20, 2022. https://therideshareguy.com/uber-statistics/.

Manyika, James. 2022. "Our Commitment on Using AI to Accelerate Progress on Global Development Goals." *Google* (blog). September 15, 2022. https://blog.google/outreach-initiatives/google-org/our-commitment-on-using-ai-to-accelerate-progress-on-global-development-goals/.

Molla, Rani. 2021. "Poll: Most Americans Want to Break up Big Tech." *Vox*, January 26, 2021. https://www.vox.com/2021/1/26/22241053/antitrust-google-facebook-break-up-big-tech-monopoly.

Merriam-Webster.com. n.d. "troglodyte." Accessed March 3, 2023. https://www.merriam-webster.com/dictionary/troglodyte.

Waters, Richard. 2014. "FT Interview with Google Co-Founder and CEO Larry Page." *Financial Times,* October 31, 2014. https://www.ft.com/content/3173f19e-5fbc-11e4-8c27-00144feabdc0.

10: BIG BROTHER

Brewster, Thomas. 2018 "Feds Force Suspect to Unlock an Apple iPhone X with Their Face." *Forbes*, October 1, 2018. https://www.forbes.com/sites/thomasbrewster/2018/09/30/feds-force-suspect-to-unlock-apple-iphone-x-with-their-face/?sh=c83b56212597.

Conger, Kate, Richard Fausset, and Serge F. Kovaleski. 2019. "San Francisco Bans Facial Recognition Technology." *The New York Times*, May 14, 2019. https://www.nytimes.com/2019/05/14/us/facial-recognition-ban-san-francisco.html.

Crockford, Kade. 2019. "What You Need to Know about Face Surveillance." Filmed November 2019 in Cambridge, Massachusetts. TED video, 12:40. https://www.ted.com/talks/kade_crockford_what_you_need_to_know_about_face_surveillance/transcript.

Gershgorn, Dave. 2021. "Is There Any Way out of Clearview's Facial Recognition Database?" *The Verge*, June 9, 2021. https://www.theverge.com/22522486/clearview-ai-facial-recognition-avoid-escape-privacy.

Heikkilä, Melissa. 2022. "The Walls Are Closing in on Clearview AI." *MIT Technology Review*, May 25, 2022. https://www.technologyreview.com/2022/05/24/1052653/clearview-ai-data-privacy-uk/.

Hill, Kashmir. 2021. "What Happens When Our Faces Are Tracked Everywhere We Go?" *The New York Times*, March 18, 2021. https://www.nytimes.com/interactive/2021/03/18/magazine/facial-recognition-clearview-ai.html.

Hill, Kashmir. 2020. "Wrongfully Accused by an Algorithm." *The New York Times*, June 24, 2020. https://www.nytimes.com/2020/06/24/technology/facial-recognition-arrest.html.

Huddleston, Cameron. 2023. "Can Life Insurance Companies Get Your Genetic Test Results?" *Forbes*, January 10, 2023. https://www.forbes.com/advisor/life-insurance/genetic-testing/.

Lomas, Natasha. 2021. "European Parliament Backs Ban on Remote Biometric Surveillance." *Yahoo!*, October 6, 2021. https://www.yahoo.com/now/european-parliament-backs-ban-remote-111017178.html

Metz, Cade, and Natasha Singer. 2018. "Newspaper Shooting Shows Widening Use of Facial Recognition by Authorities." *The New York Times*, June 29, 2018. https://www.nytimes.com/2018/06/29/business/newspaper-shooting-facial-recognition.html.

Nott, George. 2019. "Casino Facial Recognition Tech Foils Problem Gambler in Disguise." *CIO*, March 20, 2019. https://www.cio.com/article/201795/casino-facial-recognition-tech-foils-problem-gambler-in-disguise.html.

O'Murchu, Cynthia. 2021. "Facial Recognition Cameras Arrive in UK School Canteens." *The Irish Times*, October 21, 2021. https://www.irishtimes.com/business/innovation/facial-recognition-cameras-arrive-in-uk-school-canteens-1.4704506.

Peaslee, Emma. 2021. "Massachusetts Pioneers Rules for Police Use of Facial Recognition Tech." *NPR*, May 7, 2021. https://www.npr.org/2021/05/07/982709480/massachusetts-pioneers-rules-for-police-use-of-facial-recognition-tech.

Ratcliffe, Jonathan. 2022. "How Many CCTV Cameras Are There in London?" *cctv.co.uk* (blog). October 25, 2022. https://www.cctv.co.uk/how-many-cctv-cameras-are-there-in-london.

Robitzski, Dan. 2019. "Apple Patented Facial Recognition to Unlock Your Car." *Futurism*, February 12, 2019. https://futurism.com/apple-facial-recognition-car.

Sauer, Pjotr. 2021. "Privacy Fears as Moscow Metro Rolls Out Facial Recognition Pay System." *The Guardian*, October 15, 2021. https://www.theguardian.com/world/2021/oct/15/privacy-fears-moscow-metro-rolls-out-facial-recognition-pay-system.

Simonite, Tom. 2022. "This App Can Diagnose Rare Diseases from a Child's Face." *Wired*, March 8, 2022. https://www.wired.com/story/app-diagnose-rare-diseases-childs-face.

Statt, Nick. 2017. "China Is Fighting Toilet Paper Thieves with Facial Recognition Software." *The Verge*, March 20, 2017. https://www.theverge.com/2017/3/20/14986640/china-toilet-paper-theft-facial-recognition-machine.

Stolyarov, Gleb, and Gabrielle Tétrault-Farber. 2021. "'Face Control': Russian Police Go Digital against Protesters." *Reuters*, February 11, 2021. https://www.reuters.com/article/us-russia-politics-navalny-tech-idUSKBN2AB1U2.

Whittaker, Zack. 2021. "Despite Controversies and Bans, Facial Recognition Startups Are Flush with VC Cash." *TechCrunch*, July 26, 2021. https://techcrunch.com/2021/07/26/facial-recognition-flush-with-cash.

Woodhams, Samuel. 2021. "London's Met Police Is Expanding Its Use of Facial Recognition Technology." *Wired UK*, September 27, 2021. https://www.wired.co.uk/article/met-police-facial-recognition-new.

11: AI SNAKE OIL

Boykis, Vicki. 2019. "The Curse of Being Big on the Internet." *Normcore Tech* (blog). October 11, 2019. https://vicki.substack.com/p/the-curse-of-being-big-on-the-internet.

Frankfurt, Harry G. 2005. *On Bullshit*. Princeton: Princeton University Press.

Graber, Cynthia. 2007. "Snake Oil Salesmen Were onto Something." *Scientific American*, November 1, 2007. https://www.scientificamerican.com/article/snake-oil-salesmen-knew-something/.

Hulette, Doug. 2021. "How to Recognize AI Snake Oil." Princeton University, January 22, 2021. https://www.cs.princeton.edu/news/how-recognize-ai-snake-oil.

Kelnar, David. 2019. "The State of AI 2019: Divergence." MMC Ventures, March 5, 2019. https://www.stateofai2019.com/.

Nijhuis, Michelle. 2017. "How to Call BS on Big Data: A Practical Guide." *The New Yorker*, June 3, 2017. https://www.newyorker.com/tech/annals-of-technology/how-to-call-bullshit-on-big-data-a-practical-guide.

Olson, Parmy. 2019. "Nearly Half of All 'AI Startups' Are Cashing in on Hype."
Forbes, March 5, 2019.
https://www.forbes.com/sites/parmyolson/2019/03/04/nearly-half-of-all-ai-
startups-are-cashing-in-on-hype/?sh=3271c32ed022.

Purnell, Newley. 2019. "AI Startup Boom Raises Questions of Exaggerated Tech
Savvy." *The Wall Street Journal*, August 15, 2019.
https://www.wsj.com/articles/ai-startup-boom-raises-questions-of-
exaggerated-tech-savvy-11565775004.

Raghavan, Manish, Solon Barocas, Jon Kleinberg, and Karen Levy. 2019.
"Mitigating Bias in Algorithmic Hiring: Evaluating Claims and Practices."
Computer Science (June).
https://doi.org/10.48550/arXiv.1906.09208.

Schulze, Elizabeth. 2019. "40% of AI Start-Ups in Europe Have Almost Nothing
to Do with AI, Research Finds." *CNBC*, March 6, 2019.
https://www.cnbc.com/2019/03/06/40-percent-of-ai-start-ups-in-europe-not-
related-to-ai-mmc-report.html.

12: TAP THE BRAKES

American Civil Liberties Union. 2021. "Kade Crockford Bio." May 20, 2021.
https://www.aclu.org/bio/kade-crockford.

Hill, Kashmir. 2021. "What Happens When Our Faces Are Tracked Everywhere
We Go?" *The New York Times*, March 18, 2021.
https://www.nytimes.com/interactive/2021/03/18/magazine/facial-
recognition-clearview-ai.html.

Mac, Ryan, and Kashmir Hill. 2022. "Clearview AI Settles Suit and Agrees to
Limit Sales of Facial Recognition Database." *The New York Times*, May 9, 2022.
https://www.nytimes.com/2022/05/09/technology/clearview-ai-suit.html.

O'Reilly, Tim. 2019. "The Fundamental Problem with Silicon Valley's Favorite
Growth Strategy." *Quartz*, February 5, 2019.
https://qz.com/1540608/the-problem-with-silicon-valleys-obsession-with-
blitzscaling-growth.

www.ingramcontent.com/pod-product-compliance
Lightning Source LLC
Chambersburg PA
CBHW071322140726
47996CB00005B/1774